IMAGES OF THE PA

COAL MINE DISASTERS IN THE MODERN ERA c.1900–1980

Mines Rescue Service vehicle from the Selby station on display at the Apedale Heritage Centre museum, Staffordshire.

The centrepiece of the Welsh National and Universal (colliery) Mining Memorial Garden at Senghenydd is a superb life-size sculpture showing a rescue worker aiding a survivor after a disaster. The bronze statue was created by Les Johnson (www.lesjohnsonsculptor.com) and the memorial site was opened in 2013 on the 100th anniversary of the largest disaster in British mining history, when 440 men and boys lost their lives. Courtesy of Les Johnson

IMAGES OF THE PAST

COAL MINE DISASTERS IN THE MODERN ERA 1900–1980

Brian Elliott

First published in Great Britain in 2017 by
PEN & SWORD HISTORY
an imprint of
Pen & Sword Books Ltd,
47 Church Street,
Barnsley,
South Yorkshire
S70 2AS

A CIP record for this book is available from the British Library.

ISBN 978 147385 884 8

Typeset by CHIC GRAPHICS

Printed and bound by CPI Group (UK) Ltd, Croydon, CR0 4YY

Pen & Sword Books Ltd incorporates the imprints of Pen & Sword Archaeology, Atlas, Aviation, Battleground, Discovery, Family History, History, Maritime, Military, Naval, Politics, Railways, Select, Social History, Transport, True Crime, Claymore Press, Frontline Books, Leo Cooper, Praetorian Press, Remember When, Seaforth Publishing and Wharncliffe.

For a complete list of Pen & Sword titles please contact
Pen & Sword Books Limited
47 Church Street, Barnsley, South Yorkshire, S70 2AS, England
E-mail: enquiries@pen-and-sword.co.uk
Website: www.pen-and-sword.co.uk

Contents

Foreword by Ceri Thompson, Curator, Big Pit: National Coal Mining Museum (Wales) 7

Preface 8

Chapter One
1900–1909: Over a Thousand Deaths a Year 9

Chapter Two
1910–1919: '... Poor Lads Left in the Ground' 31

Chapter Three
1920–1929: '... The Sad Bells of Rhymney' 49

Chapter Four
1930–1939: The 'Wicked Thirties' 67

Chapter Five
1940–1949: War to Nationalisation 89

Chapter Six
1950–1959: A Great Escape and the Last Major Disasters 111

Chapter Seven
1960–1969: South Wales, Silverwood and Scotland 133

Chapter Eight
1970–1979: Britain's Last Pit Disasters: Remembering Lofthouse and Safety in Mines 151

Endpiece 173

Sources and Credits 174

This local postcard image, published by A & G Taylor after the West Stanley disaster of 1909, features 'Billy' Gardner 'the boy who risked his life to save his pit pony'. Purchasers of the card are also informed – via the inscription – that 'the pony has been presented to him by Mr Burns' (one of the pit's owners).

Foreword

The coalmining disaster has always excited the imagination of both the media and the general public. Coalminers, who were portrayed as 'The Enemy Within' when they fought for better wages and conditions, magically became 'Brave British Heroes' when involved in rescuing comrades trapped by explosions and floods.

Between 1851 and 1920 there were forty-eight disasters in the south Wales coalfield alone with over 3,000 deaths (a third of the total UK figure). In fact, the worst disaster in UK mining history took place at The Universal Colliery, Senghenydd with 439 men (and a rescue man) being killed. Therefore, disasters have been a major part of museum interpretation at Big Pit. In fact I have only recently concluded an oral history project on the Cambrian Colliery explosion of 1965.

It is in this light that I welcome Brian Elliott's well-illustrated and researched book on twentieth-century mining disasters.

Ceri Thompson, Curator, Big Pit: National Coal Museum (Wales)

Preface

Although disaster deaths accounted for only a small proportion of fatalities in British mines, they attracted a great deal of media attention throughout the 20th century, not only through newspapers but via radio broadcasts and cinema news film. It was the disasters that were the main catalysts for new regulation and legislation that made the coal industry a far safer place to work.

Throughout this book one of the most outstanding features is the unselfish attitude and actions of miners to help trapped, injured or dead colleagues. Rescue stories and acts of bravery permeate most of the pages.

The extent and nature of the book has had to be limited because of the sheer number of disasters that took place during the century, especially before 1950. Each of the 'mega' disasters: National (1901), West Stanley (1909), Wellington (1910), Pretoria (1910), Universal (1913), Minnie (1918), Gresford (1934) and William (1947), were so massive that many thousands of words could have been added to already bulging bibliographies. It has been impossible to cover every single disaster but the overview presented at the start of each decade provides a context for the era.

By 'disaster', I have used '5-plus fatalities' in a single event (allowing for deaths days afterwards) as my main starting point, rather than the nine or ten figure used, often arbitrarily so, elsewhere.

Much appreciation is due to a variety of individuals and organisations for the use of illustrative material (see page 174). Special thanks however must go to Ceri Thompson, Curator at the Big Pit (National Coal Museum: Wales) for writing the Foreword and for always being on hand for my many queries and requests; and thanks also to the library staff at the National Coal Mining Museum for England, for their efficiency and kindness and the use of the research facilities there. Les Johnson was kind enough to let me use an image of his 'rescuer' sculpture at the Senghenydd memorial site; as was Ray Johnson MBE for a Staffordshire Film Archive item. Thanks, also, to Margaret Crosby, Whitehaven News and to ex-miners Tony Banks and Aidan Bell.

> 'They stood on the pavement for a few seconds rehearsing what they were going to say, before Alf knocked on the door. There was a pause, then Alf cleared his throat and took off his cap when he heard the bolts being withdrawn at the other side.': Barry Hines, *The Price of Coal* (1979)

Chapter One

1900-1909
Over a Thousand Deaths a Year

At the start of the twentieth century coalmining was a booming industry, with hundreds of individual pit owners and companies doing so well that more and more labour was required. Extracting coal continued to be highly labour-intensive, manpower increasing every year: from around 759,000 in 1900 to well over a million (1,010,00) in 1909. Annual output in the same period rose from less than 220 to around 267 million tons; but it was achieved at an enormous human cost.

Each year well over a thousand miners lost their lives in 'everyday accidents', a dreadful carnage that soared to 1,453 fatalities by 1909. The vast majority of these, about 93%, involved individual or occasionally very small numbers (2-4) of men and boys who lost their lives in the process of getting or transporting the coal underground. Thus, 'disasters', multiple-fatality accidents involving five or more deaths, formed only a small proportion of the toll, even less so, around 5%, in relation to 'major' or 'principal' disasters involving ten or more fatalities.

But it was the disasters that caused such traumatic, widespread and lasting damage to families and mining communities, they remained in the personal and public memory for generations; and, thanks to memorials and events, many of them continue to be commemorated today.

Wales, especially in the valleys, was very badly affected, miners there working the gaseous and highly inflammable steam coal that was so prized the world over. Between 1900 and 1909 almost two out of three 'over 5-death' disasters were located in Wales. Together, and in rank order, the coalfields of Lancashire, Scotland and Durham accounted for the rest.

One of the worst disasters of the new century occurred in the old mining county of Durham, at West Stanley in 1909; and a series of major disasters (see table below) attracted widespread news coverage and a mixture of condemnation and concern from the public especially from the miners' unions.

'Explosions' were the main kind of disasters recorded by the mines inspectors and coroners, accounting for more than half of the very serious incidents. Associated with them were emissions of gas, and post-explosion 'afterdamp', often the major cause of deaths. But horrendous multiple-fatality accidents involving falls down the shaft during sinking operations or engine winding were not uncommon.

For every disaster there were reports of extraordinary acts of courage and bravery, including those involving miners who volunteered as rescue workers. A variety of awards were presented, but the most notable example was the Edward Medal for Mines, instituted by royal warrant on 13 July 1907, often referred to as the 'miners' VC'.

Although not yet required by law, the first decade of the new century was a time when a mines rescue service began to operate from a small number of bases or stations. The first, in 1902, opened in a purpose-built brick house near Barnsley (known as the 'Tankersley' station). Others gradually followed, strategically placed among pits in the major coalfields, at Howe Bridge (Lancashire, 1908); Wath upon Dearne (Yorkshire, 1908); Abercam and Crumlin (Wales, 1909); Mansfield (Nottinghamshire, 1909); Altofts (Yorkshire, 1909); Elswick (County Durham, 1909); and Cowdenbeath (Fife, 1909).

The new stations were where teams of men were trained in the use of rescue techniques and especially in the use of self-contained breathing apparatus. The early 'brigades' are often portrayed in photographs using Draeger, WEG (see below) or Meco-Briggs equipment; but a pioneering British company, Siebe Gorman (SG), a specialist manufacturer of deep-sea breathing apparatus, became the market leader. From 1907, SG's young engineer Robert Davies improved the older Fluess apparatus and developed a much more reliable and efficient 'industrial rebreather', which was given the brand-name 'Proto'.

Miners' MPs and miners' leaders continued to press for improved 'safety in mines' legislation. The union men were especially passionate for urgent change when speaking at inquiries, meetings and galas. In 1906, parliament's response was the appointment of a royal commission on accidents in mines.

A new research body, the Safety in Mines Establishment, began work in 1908, carrying out experiments in coal dust explosions in the west Yorkshire village of Altofts, in William Edward Garforth's West Riding Colliery. A key figure in mines rescue at this time, Garforth (1845-1921), elected as President of the British Miners' Association in 1907, introduced improved breathing apparatus, known as 'WEG' after his initials.

In 1909, the second report of the royal commission dealt with ventilation, falls of ground, haulage and shaft accidents; and a parliamentary select committee was appointed to investigate mining accidents.

A remarkable innovator, John Scott Haldane (1860-1936), not only visited pits after disasters (in order to evaluate the nature of the post-explosion gas) but also carried out gas inhalation experiments on himself. The intrepid Dr Haldane was able to identify carbon monoxide in the 'afterdamp', the toxic and invisible gas that accounted for so many miners' deaths after explosions. From the 1890s it was Haldane who introduced the idea and the use of canaries (and occasionally mice) as the most sensitive 'detectors' of gas; and even invented a safe 'canary box' for the birds, in which oxygen was released for their revival. Haldane's contribution was enormously important, and in turn valued, as canaries continued to be kept and used in mines right up to the 1980s.

The thirty HM mines inspectors did what they could to deal with accidents and disasters in their respective regions but were woefully over stretched, unable to fully investigate and monitor safety issues and working practices concerning over 2,700 collieries. By 1909, the annual average fatal accident rate per thousand employed underground remained high, at 1.453% or one death for every 699 miners. Put another way, there were at least four fatalities in British mines *every work day*; and at this time (1909) more than a third (1,453) of all (4,133) industrial fatal accidents in Britain concerned miners (*British Labour Statistics: Historical Abstract 1886-1968* [1971]).

Although in the 1900s miners were safer than their counterparts of two or more generations earlier, there remained the ever present probability of a wife or mother not seeing their loved one at the end of a working day, through accidental death or serious injury. Disasters, though terrible, provided at least one almost comforting though by no means acceptable difference: a shared sense of communal loss. But try vocalising that in a household where one or more of its family members were lost: father and son or sons; or brothers in arms. For some, bereavement was incomplete where bodies of their loved ones were never recovered.

Silver medal presented to S.Hughes of Woolley Colliery Ambulance Brigade (Yorkshire), 'for attendance at drill during 1902'.

Timeline of coal mine disaster fatalities (5+), 1900-1909

29 June 1900: **Old Boston**, Haydock, Lancashire: (sinking) 8

17 August 1900: **Portland (No.5)**, Ayr, Ayrshire: (explosion) 6

24 October 1900: **Glenavon**, Croeserw, Glamorganshire: (inrush) 5

15 February 1901: **Hill of Beath**, Fife, Fifeshire: (fire): 7

24 May 1901: **Universal,** Senghenydd, Glamorganshire: (explosion) 81

26 August 1901: **Donibristle**, Fife, Fifeshire: (inrush) 8

10 September 1901: **Llanbradach**, Llanbranach, Glamorgan: (explosion) 8

4 December 1901: **Kemberton**, Shifnal, Staffordshire: (winding) 6

4 March 1902: **Milfraen**, Blaenavon, Monmouthshire: (winding) 5

2 April 1902: **Garswood Hall**, Ashton, Lancashire: (sinking) 8

3 June 1902: **Windsor**, Abertridwr, Glamorganshire: (sinking) 6

4 June 1902: **Fochriw (No.2)**, Dowlais, Glamorganshire: (explosion) 8

3 September 1902: **McLaren (No.1)**, Abertysswg, Glamorganshire: (explosion) 17

1 October 1902: **Tirpentwys**, Pontypool, Monmouthshire: (winding) 8

11 November 1902: **Ocean (Deep Navigation)**, Treharris, Glamorganshire: (winding) 5

27 July 1904: **Aldwarke Main**, Rotherham, Yorkshire: (winding): 6

13 August 1904: **Nine Mile Point**, Cwmfelinfach, Monmouthshire: (sinking) 7

21 January 1905: **Elba**, Gowerton, Glamorganshire: (explosion) 11

20 January 1905: **Bold**, St Helens, Lancashire: (winding) 5

10 March 1905: **Cambrian**, Clydach, Glamorganshire: (explosion) 33

11 July 1905: **National**, Wattsdown, Glamorganshire: (explosion) 119

16 July 1905: **New Boston**, Haydock, Lancashire: (roof fall) 5

28 April 1906: **Dowlais,** Abercynon, Glamorganshire: (haulage) 5

1 June 1906: **Court Herbert**, Neath, Glamorganshire: (explosion) 5

14 October 1906: **Wingate Grange,** Wingate, Durham: (explosion) 26

10 November 1906: **Albion**, Cilfynydd, Glamorganshire: (explosion) 6

16 February 1907: **Timsharan** (Waunhir), Kidwelly, Carmarthen: (haulage) 6

5 March 1907: **Genwen**, Llanelli, Carmarthen: (explosion) 6

4 October 1907: **Foggs**, Tyldesley, Lancashire: (winding) 10

10 November 1907: **Seven Sisters**, Dulais Valley, Glamorganshire: (explosion) 5

15 November 1907: **Barrow**, Barnsley, Yorkshire: (winding) 7

26 November 1907: **William,** Whitehaven, Cumberland: (explosion) 5

14 December 1907: **Dinas Main**, Gilfach Goch, Glamorganshire: (explosion) 7

20 February 1908: **Glebe**, Washington, Durham: (explosion) 14

4 March 1908: **Hamstead**, Great Barr, Staffordshire: (fire) 26

9 April 1908: **Norton Hill**, Midsomer Norton, Somerset: (explosion) 10

18 August 1908: **Maypole**, Abram, Lancashire: (explosion) 75

16 February 1909: **West Stanley**, West Stanley, Durham: (explosion) 168

3 August 1909: **Bersham,** Wrexham: (explosion) 9

27 August 1909: **Naval (Ely pit)**, Penycraig, Glamorganshire: (winding) 6

1 October 1909: **Birchrock**, Pontardulais, Glamorganshire: (explosion) 7

29 October 1909: **Darran**, Deri, Glamorganshire: (explosion) 27

1 November 1909: **Tareni**, Godregraig, Glamorganshire: (inrush) 5

10 December 1909: **Caprington No. 4**, Ayr, Ayrshire: (inrush) 10

Pit sinking was a precarious occupation, the workers having to cope with inrushes of water, gas emissions and explosions; as well as falls down the shaft. Being part of a sinking team was a highly specialist and itinerant way of life, often involving many months of work before moving on to a new site. The sinkers, wearing distinctive oilskins, are occasionally pictured in early postcard images. This example relates to the Victoria pit, only about a mile from Barnsley town centre. Four men have crammed themselves into a sinking bucket, or 'hoppit' as they were known, perhaps to please the requirements of the photographer, maybe to celebrate the reaching of the Barnsley coal. The sinker-teams were often formed as off-shoots of mining engineering firms or as separate concerns, all under the leadership of a 'master sinker'.

Winding/Shaft Accidents

Almost sixty men and boys were killed in nine very serious (five-plus fatally) winding accidents during a short period, from 1901 to 1909. The cage mishap at Shifnal in Staffordshire in 1901 was the start of a dreadful sequence. South Wales was badly affected, with three winding disasters in a single year (1902): at Milfraen, Tirpentwys and Ocean (Deep Navigation) collieries; and in 1909 six lives were lost in a terrible incident at Naval Colliery in the Rhondda. In Lancashire there were two winding accidents, at Bold (1905) and Foggs pits (1907); and two more in south Yorkshire, at Aldwarke Main (1904) and Barrow Colliery (1907).

These disasters usually involved the 'cages' in which the men were travelling up or down the shaft crashing at speed (after detaching from suspension chains or ropes) or jerking so suddenly during winding that the occupants were thrown out. Amazingly, some miners survived from such horrific 'rides': thirteen for instance at Bold (1905) when the out of control cage was saved from hitting the pit bottom when it smashed into a wooden sinking platform. Three of the five fatalities were boys of only 14 years old and another was just 15. The five miners killed in the Milfraen incident, were flung out of the cage during winding, falling to the bottom of the shaft. The deceased included two 'collier boys' aged 13 and another lad aged 15. The Foggs colliery accident was actually a collision in the shaft between the ascending and descending cages, the routine clearance between them when they 'met' said to be only three-and-a-half inches. At Ocean Colliery, twenty-five day-shift men had a fortunate escape when ascending at the end of their stint, a broken pipe and the water it normally conveyed smashed through the double-decked cage, killing four men and fatally injuring another who had been thrown out. It took six hours to get the men back to the surface. The Naval (Ely Pit) winding disaster was a particularly harrowing one, twenty-two men and boys may have escaped death but most of them received terrible injuries; and goodness knows what their mental state must have been like afterwards, and maybe for the rest of their lives.

The regional mines inspectors reported in some detail regarding the cause or causes of 'disasters that should not have happened' and on their safety implications. The cages themselves varied a great deal from pit to pit and region to region, sometimes, as at Barrow for example, little more than crude timber containers with no safety gates. Although 'accidental death' was the most common outcome of coroner's juries, in the case of Barrow two shaftmen men were found guilty of 'great carelessness and negligence', though not criminally so.

The Barrow cage mishap occurred when the winding engine man at the pit top, after receiving a signal from the onsetter (pit bottom cage operative), started raising the cage after a man had disembarked at a landing. But the cage was still attached to the side of the shaft and therefore swung so violently on its ascent that seven of the sixteen occupants were flung out, falling to certain death in the pit bottom. Two 'hangers-on' on the landing were deemed responsible of 'carelessness and negligence' as they had left a 'flat-sheet' (stepping platform) still in place. Several postcard images relating to the Barrow disaster appeared immediately afterwards, this one a typical montage assembled by one of the most enterprising of all the Edwardian photographic firms, Warner Gothard of Barnsley.

The small, double-decked Barrow cage as it appeared as a drawing in the mines inspector's report and *Colliery Guardian*. The miners only had single 'holding in' chains for protection when ascending and descending the shaft.

When the double-decked cage at the Ely pit of Naval Colliery, Penygraig, containing twenty-eight men increased speed during winding towards the end of its descent, on 27 August 1909, the experienced engineman at the surface applied the reversing spanner which duly broke in the process. Consequently, the cage crashed into the the beams protecting the sump in the pit bottom; and the empty ascending cage shot upwards into the headgear, then plummeted downwards (its rope having snapped), smashing into the the top of the pit bottom cage full of men, and jamming it into the sump. The upper deck occupants fared worst by the massive impact, four or five killed instantly and another so badly injured that he died shortly afterwards. This artist's impression of the scene was created for the *Illustrated Police News*.

Inrushes and Inundations

Inrushes of water were an ever-present danger for miners, especially in the shallower pits, in awkward geological conditions and in areas where there were old workings. As with all disasters, great crowds rushed to the pit heads when news broke. Being trapped underground was an outcome that caused great distress for all concerned and made search, rescue and recovery attempts extremely difficult and dangerous.

There were four very serious 'inundations' in the early 1900s: two in south Wales, at Glenavon in the Rhondda (1900) and Tareni in the Swansea Valley (1909); and two in Scotland, at Donibristle (1901) and Caprington (1909). Also, at the Union Colliery in the Forest of Dean in 1902, four miners, including two brothers, lost their lives following a sudden inrush of water. Three men were found to be still alive and taken to the surface by a persistent rescue party after *five* days of 'entombment'.

At Donibristle, an inflow of 'moss' (liquified peat), from moorland above the mine, burst into a heading in the Mynheer seam resulting in the deaths of the two miners who had been probing upwards with a rod, in order to create an air shaft. Two other men working in the lower part of the mine were drowned and six more trapped. A four-man rescue team were also lost when attempting to access the trapped miners. Five of the trapped men were freed the next day but recovery of the sixth person was more difficult, two of the rescuers themselves became trapped by a further inrush of moss, though eventually freed by the heroic efforts of Baillie John Sheddon. Five of the bodies were found three months after the disaster, their desperate plight made evident in the recovery of a notebook containing frail entries, including their 'last goodbyes'.

An inrush of surface water during the night at the Caprington mine, near Kilmarnock, was so powerful that it flooded the workings and resulted in the deaths of ten miners, aged between 15 and 36.

The five miners who were drowned in the Glenavon pit, were advancing a face when water burst through the roof. Eighty others managed to escape via the upcast shaft.

At the Tareni pit (a drift mine), Godregraig, water from an adjacent old mine gushed down the main roadway resulting in the deaths of five miners, including Ben Griffiths, aged 14, on his first day underground. Another boy of the same age, Evan Harris, also perished. The rest of the shift of about a hundred men managed to escape by wading through the rushing water that at times reached their waists.

Searchers under the flickering lights of a string of naphtha (oil) lamps returning at 2 am with the last three survivors taken from the Donibristle mine, near Cowdenbeath. This engraving by Charles M. Sheldon, featured on the front page of the weekly news magazine *Black and White*, captures the dramatic event more graphically than a photographical image could have done. Note the exhausted expression on the face of the first escorted survivor, and the anxious crowd stretching away towards a moonlit horizon.

In 1900, the south Wales village of Senghenydd, in the Aber Valley near Caerphilly, was fast developing, incomers attracted by work at the Universal Colliery. But on 24 May 1901, at about 5.10 am, a violent explosion swept through the mine, killing all but one (William Harris, a haulier, whose horse was found dead beside him) of the remaining night shift men: 81 men and boys. Many of the bodies were so badly mutilated and burnt that bereaved families were advised to bury their loved ones 'unseen'.

Detail (above) from four of the ceramic name tiles relating to the victims of the 1901 disaster (created by Ned Heywood and Julia Land) that form part of the wall of remembrance around the central statue at the new (October, 2013) Welsh National and Universal Mining Memorial Garden, at Senghenydd.

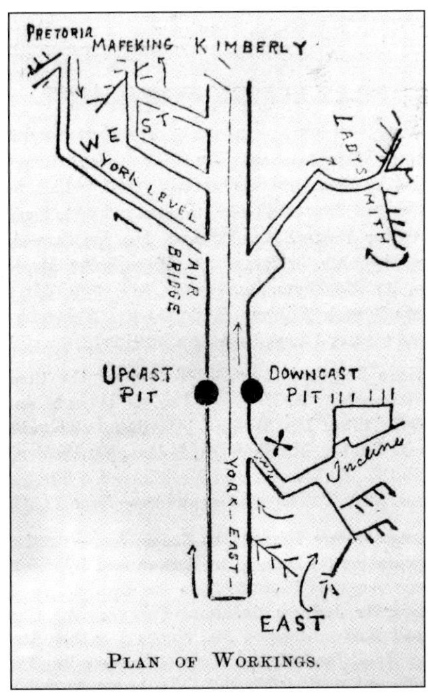

A sketch-map of the underground workings at the time of the disaster.

UNIVERSAL COLLIERY
Senghenydd

24th May • Mai 1901
81 Fatalities • Marwolaethau

14th October • Hedref 1913
440 Fatalities • Marwolaethau

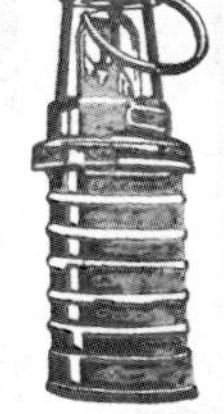

Sponsored by • Noddwyd gan
Caerphilly County Borough
Council • A.W.Abraham

ELBA COLLIERY
Gowerton

21st January • Ionawr 1905
11 Fatalities • Marwolaethau

Sponsored by • Noddwyd gan
Coalfields Regeneration
Trust

CAMBRIAN COLLIERY
Clydach Vale, Rhondda

10th March • Mawrth 1905
33 Fatalities • Marwolaethau

17th May • Mai 1965
31 Fatalities • Marwolaethau

Sponsored by
Noddwyd gan
Rhondda Cynon Taff

NATIONAL COLLIERY
Wattstown, Rhondda

11th July • Gorffennaf 1905
119 Fatalities • Marwolaethau

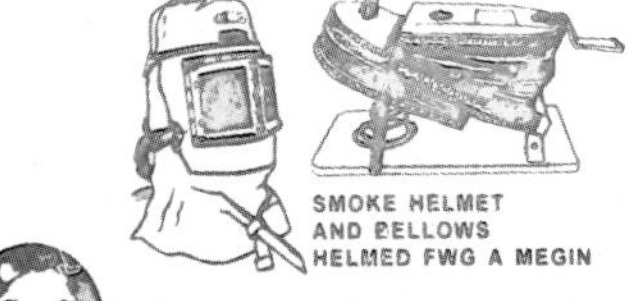

Sponsored by
Noddwyd gan
Rhondda Cynon Taff

As already noted, Wales fared very badly for mine disasters during the early 1900s, particularly from explosions. The montage of images here are but a small selection of the tiles forming a 'path of memory' at the Welsh National and Universal Mining Memorial Garden. Walking by these and the individual Senghenydd 'victim' tiles should not fail to make the visitor aware of the great sacrifice made by Welsh miners, their families and communities.

DARRAN COLLIERY
Deri

29th October • Hedref 1909
27 Fatalities • Marwolaethau

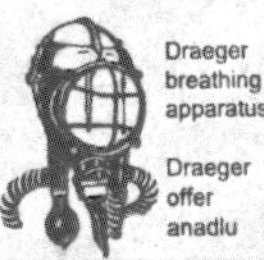

Sponsored by • Noddwyd gan
Caerphilly County Borough
Council

1905 was a particularly terrible year for miners and their families associated with two Glamorganshire collieries. The explosion at about 6.15 pm in the Cambrian Colliery, at Clydach Vale in the Rhondda, on 10 March accounted for the deaths of thirty-three men and boys, many of them dreadfully burnt, making identification far from easy. Two of the bodies were never recovered, believed to have been incinerated in the haulage engine house. The chief mines inspector for the Cardiff district, Fred Gray, was convinced that the use of a thinly protected (single rather than double gauze) Clanny lamp was the source of the ignition. Four months later, on 11 July, a huge explosion occurred late morning at another Rhondda mine, in the No. 2 pit of the United National Colliery, Wattsdown. The 119 fatalities included the colliery general manager William Meredith. One of the most tragic aspects of the disaster was the extraordinary number of 'boy miners' who lost their lives, thirty-three of them under the age of 15. Although men and boys were found with terrible injuries from the blast, most died as a result of the poisonous 'afterdamp'.

The funeral cortege procession for the Wattsdown disaster victims was said to have been five miles long.

In England, 1908 was a black year for mining safety, with four major 'explosion/fire disasters': at Glebe (County Durham); Hamstead (Staffordshire); Norton Hill (Somerset); and Maypole (Lancashire) collieries.

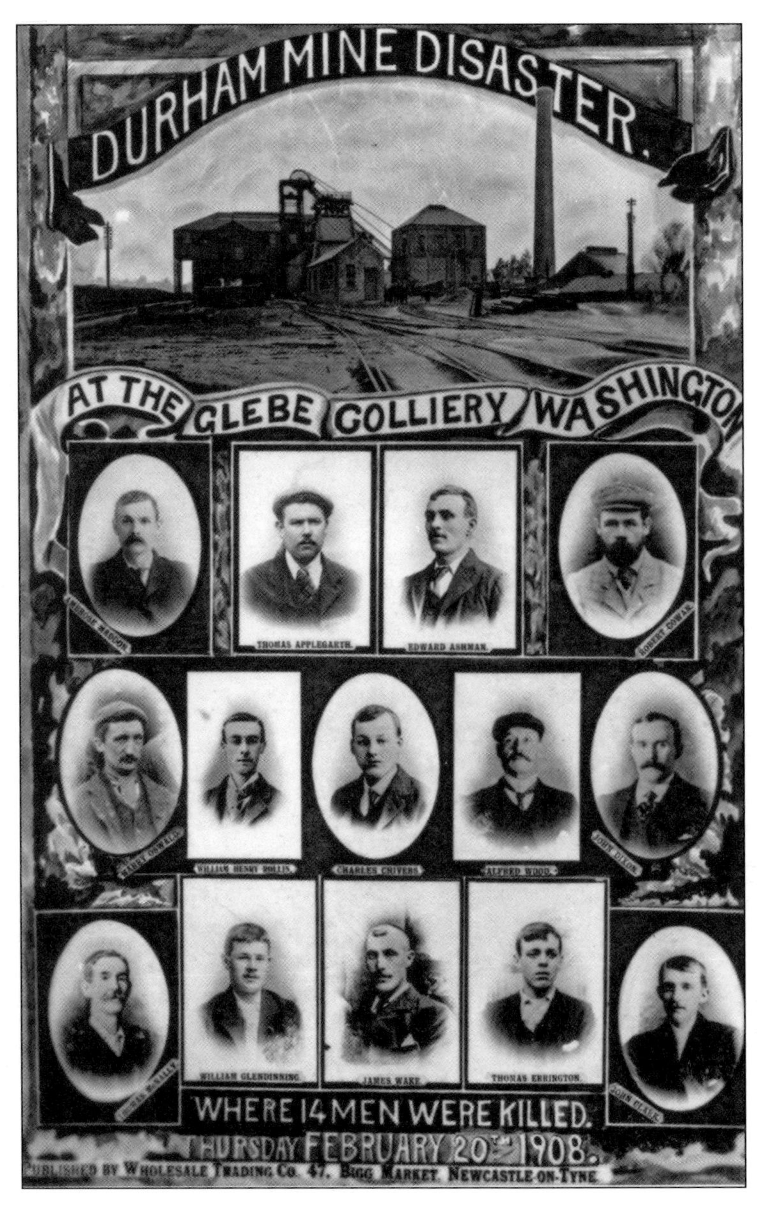

One of three photo-montage images (created by Warner Gothard of Barnsley) relating to the Glebe disaster. This example includes small portraits of each of the victims. The mine was only established a couple of years earlier, sunk through soft ground by the new shaft-freezing process. The explosion occurred at about 9.30 in the evening, killing all but one of the fifteen men preparing for the day-shift hewers. Nine of the men were said to have died directly from the shock of the blast; and the others from the afterdamp.

Perhaps the most significant of all of the early twentieth-century disasters concerned the very serious underground fire (and its deadly aftermath) that engulfed Hamstead Colliery, near Great Barr, Birmingham on the night of 4 March 1908, believed to have been caused by a spark accidentally igniting a box of candles. Although the number of fatalities, twenty-six, was well below those of several other recent major disasters, the circumstances of the incident highlighted one dire need for all of the coalfields: fully trained and well-equipped rescue brigades located near to collieries.

This composite image produced as a postcard by Warner Gothard features most of the Hamstead victims and the Tankersely 'brigade rescue party'.

Although a few miners managed to escape, exploration to locate the 'entombed' remainder was hampered by highly dangerous underground conditions (dense smoke, poisoned air and roof collapses). It took almost 24 hours for two rescue teams from Yorkshire to arrive at the scene. A group of five from William Garforth's West Riding Colliery, at Altofts were equipped with WEG breathing apparatus; and a small team came from the new rescue station at Tankersley near Barnsley, with Draeger gear. Earlier, traditional methods had been used to 'test the air' in order to evaluate the underground atmosphere: the lowering of 'a rat in a basket' and 'a bird'; and on the pit top Dr John Scott Haldane did tests in the fan house in order to evaluate the 'vapour and fumes' from below, using caged mice as indicators. Unfortunately, one of the Altofts men, John Welsby, exhausted and oxygen-expired, had to be left a few hundred yards from the pit bottom, despite herculean efforts of his colleague, John Whittingham, and died at the scene. Welsby and Whitingham, along with five other rescue men were subsequently awarded the new and prestigious Edward Medal in recognition of their bravery on 5 March. Exceptionally, five of the awardees got the First Class (silver) medal.

The Altofts mines rescue team equipped with WEG breathing apparatus on their way to descend the Hamstead shaft, Welsby, one of their members never to return alive.

An explosion on the night of 9 April 1908 resulted in the deaths of ten miners at Norton Hill Colliery, part of the small Radstock coalfield in north Somerset. Pit disasters in this area may not have been of the same magnitude as elsewhere but were felt with an equal sense of loss in the close communities affected by such tragedies. Although several postcard images were issued, the photographs shown here and published in the *Colliery Guardian* are both interesting and realistic. Shown above is one of the first motor ambulances at the colliery and below, three of the volunteer rescuers in their 'everyday' mining clothes.

Photographic coverage of the Maypole Colliery (Abram, near Wigan) disaster of Tuesday, 18 August 1908, in which 75 men and boys were killed after a massive explosion, was much more extensive than at earlier tragedies. This image reproduced from the *Colliery Guardian* shows several of the grim-faced rescuers carrying their lamps, pausing at the pithead for a photographer, after a long night of searching underground. Local miners under the direction of the pit's manager, Arthur Rushton began the rescue operations. Later there was assistance within Lancashire from the men of the new Howe Bridge rescue station, at Atherton and from the experienced Altofts team from Normanton, near Wakefield.

This studio photograph was published as a postcard by Will Smith of Wigan. It shows the 'only survivors' of the Maypole disaster, presumably wearing the same attire that they wore underground, during and after their immediate escape to the surface. The three men happened to be working in a part of the mine not affected by the explosion, and were conveyed to safety by rescuers via a shaft of the adjacent Junction Colliery.

Warner Gothard produced three high quality photo-montage postcards concerning the Maypole disaster – and also a slightly revised version of the one shown here. This example includes small portraits of many of the victims and a list of the others. Unfortunately mistakes were made, the total fatalities given as 76 rather than 75 and a total of 77 names are listed. It wasn't easy getting the correct information, especially when one Maypole employee, William Moore, had failed to report at the colliery until the day after the explosion, and another, George Melling, had 'gone missing' for several days.

Tuesday, 16 February 1909 was an extremely black day for West Stanley and its colliery, known locally as 'Oakey's' and more generally as 'Burn's Pit' after its owners, J.H. and F.H. Burn. At 3.45 pm, about half an hour before the end of the day shift, a massive explosion ripped through the workings, immediately followed by another blast. Although thirty miners managed to survive, the outcome was absolutely horrendous: 168 men and boys killed. Although the vast majority lost their lives due to carbon monoxide poisoning and from 'coal dust suffocation', others died as a result of the 'direct violence' of the blasts. It was and remains Durham's worst coalmining disaster. The two rare 'press' images shown below appeared in the *Colliery Guardian*. Relatives are pictured 'waiting for news' and a large assembly of people are shown near the pithead, listening to information.

Opportunistic as ever, arriving from Barnsley, the Warner Gothard photographic firm was able to produce several composite postcards within a few days of the disaster, managing to cram in 117 head-and-shoulder portraits in this example. Among the borrowed family images used were several youngsters wearing football shirts. Nine boys aged just 13-14 lost their lives in the pit and more than a third of all the victims were under the age of twenty.

The explosion at Darran Colliery, Deri, in south Wales, on 29 October 1909 occurred towards the end of the night shift, with 45 miners still underground, the blast was so powerful that the cage plummeted down the downcast shaft. Although some miners escaped through underground roadways that connected to Gilfach Colliery, those that were badly injured and affected by carbon monoxide gas remained trapped, as did six men who insisted on staying in order to help. As the nearest mine rescue station (Aberaman) was almost 20 miles away it was left to a group of brave volunteers to find and assist any survivors. Unfortunately five of the rescuers, with minimal equipment, got overcome with the gas and perished, as did those who had stayed behind. This graphic image is part of a detailed spread about the tragedy, published in the *Illustrated Police News*. It features William Evans, a pit carpenter, who descended the upcast shaft on five occasions via a rope ladder in order to reach his stricken mates. Evans, along with Evan Owen, Edmund Davies and the village doctor, William Turner, were awarded the Edward Medal in recognition of their extreme bravery; and the valour of the 'eleven heroes' was marked by Carnegie Trust Fund awards, albeit posthumously.

Chapter Two

1910-1919

... poor lads left in the ground

(from Wilfred Owen's *The Miners*, 1918)

The demand for coal in order to drive the British economy continued to be huge during the second decade of the twentieth century; and of course coal had massive military as well as domestic importance during 1914-18, the Great War years. Employment in the industry peaked at 1.1 million in 1913 but the rush to join the colours – around 250,000 miners responding to the call to arms; and many thousands never returning alive – meant a significant fall in the size of the workforce, despite campaigns to attract men and boys into mining from all walks of life. In 1915, manpower had declined to 953,000 as tens of thousands of 'the best', the younger but highly skilled miners, had been lost to the military.

Compared with the previous ten years, the number of fatalities in the industry increased significantly during 1910-1919, averaging 1,380 a year, peaking at a dreadfully high 1,775 deaths in 1910. The wider context of this crisis is well described by the mining historian John Benson:

> Between 1868-1919 a miner was killed every six hours, seriously injured every two hours and injured badly every two or three minutes. (*British coalminers in the nineteenth century. A social history*, 1980, p.43.)

Although the number of disasters (5 or more fatality events) was far less than in the previous decade, the twenty-six that did take place included five major examples (featured in this chapter) accounting for 85% of total 'disaster deaths'. The big disasters accounted for hundreds of pages and millions of words in the regional and national press, and concerned five different coalfields: Cumberland (Wellington), Lancashire (Pretoria), Yorkshire (Cadeby) and Staffordshire (Podmore/Minnie); and in South Wales at the Universal Colliery, at Senghenydd, where 440 men and boys lost their lives in Britain's worst ever mining disaster.

Explosions and their immediate aftermaths continued to be the main type of disaster, though serious sinking and winding accidents, at Hattonrigg (Lancashire) and Water Haigh (Yorkshire); and two bad incidents in Nottinghamshire, at Rufford and Bentinck, remained

'The under-seas tomb of over a hundred men' was the dramatic headline caption used for this image, drawn by Charles De Lacy on behalf of the *Illustrated London News* (21 May 1910). Amid steam and smoke, the headgears and their timber supports, the great cupola chimney and castle-like engine house of Wellington pit are shown overlooking the harbour at Whitehaven. The embattled and crenelated buildings were designed by architect Sydney Smirk. Little now remains, apart from the iconic 'candlestick' chimney, though the winter storms of 2016 uncovered structural remnants by the shoreline.

very worrying for all concerned in the industry, especially of course the affected families and communities. Another of the miners' most dreaded happenings – inrushes of water – caused mass heartache at a Yorkshire pit (Car House) and two Lanarkshire mines (Neilsland and Stanrigg).

Among the very many safety-related innovations in the landmark Coal Mines Act of 1911 were new rules concerning safety lamps, shafts and winding, signalling, electricity, ventilation, explosives, and coal dust 'prevention'. Boys under the age of fourteen were no longer allowed to work underground. Very importantly, the mine owners, either individually or co-operatively, had the responsibility to 'make adequate provision for the safe conduct of rescue and other necessary work in mines after an explosion or a fire, or otherwise in an atmosphere which may be dangerous to life'. This meant that 'fully equipped' rescue stations

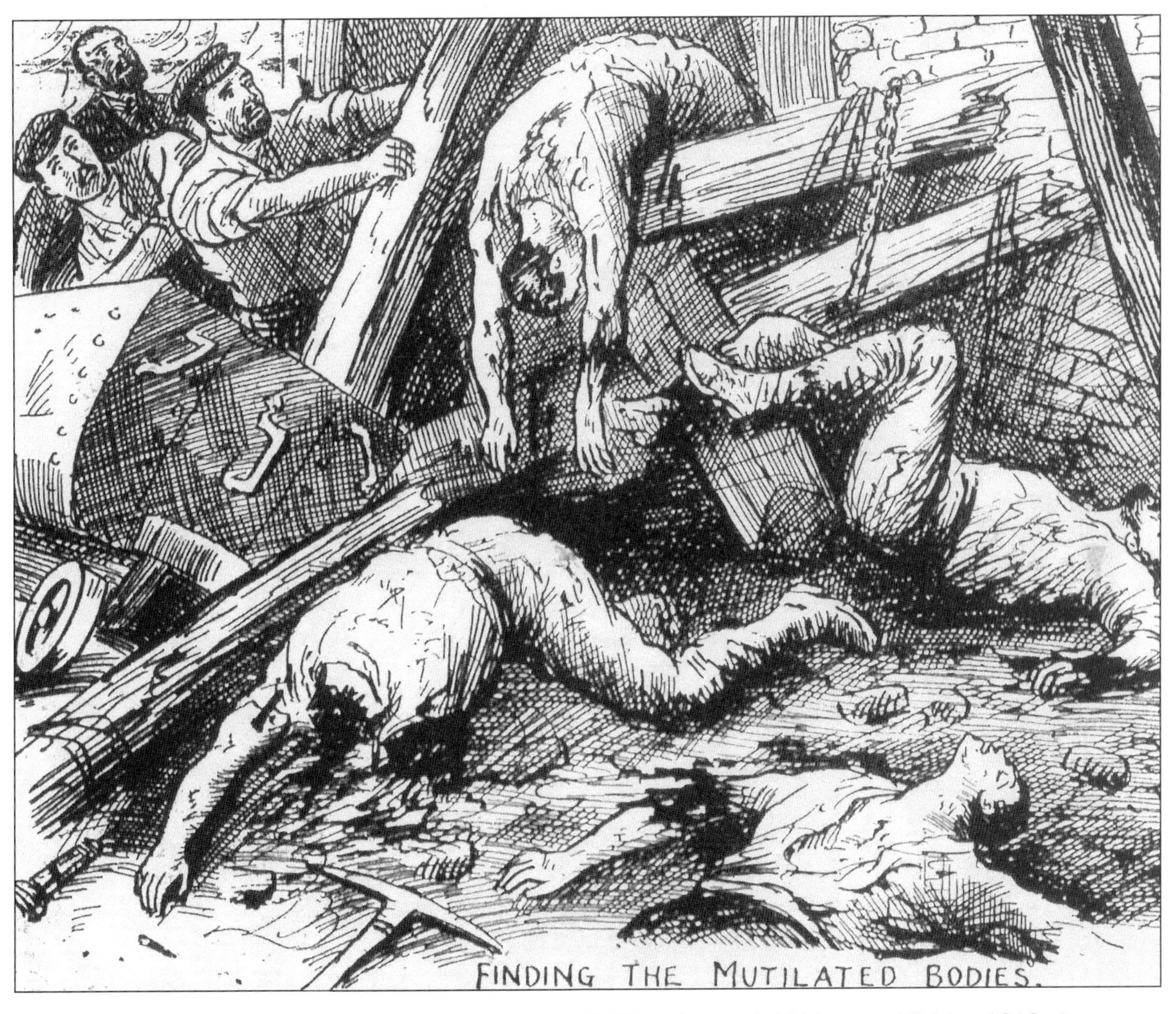

When an explosion occurred at Markham Colliery in south Wales on 18 May 1912 the force of the blast was so violent that several miners and heavy equipment were hurled many yards; and when found the bodies were described as 'terribly mutilated'.

Rescue workers recovering the badly injured miner John Snashall after a six-hour search following a massive explosion at Tredegar Iron Company's Markham Colliery in south Wales on 18 May 1912. The four rescuers: Llewllyn Howells, James Leach, Arthur Winborn and William Wooley, were awarded Edward medals for their exceptional bravery.

had to be located at 'convenient centres' – to be called Central Rescue Stations – at least 15 miles radius from most mines; and a 'permanent rescue corps' organised and maintained there. In addition, 'rescue brigades' of at least five fully-trained men had to be placed at each mine (apart from small mines), the recommended number of brigades according to the employment-size of the colliery, the largest pits requiring at least three brigades. It had taken many accidents and disasters and thousands of lives for the 'rescue station' recommendations from the Royal Commission of 1886 to be implemented.

In 1912, over a million miners, following reductions in pay and increasing poverty, went on strike in order to obtain a minimum wage but were back at work by 6 April with little achieved for all their efforts. But 1919, after numerous local and regional disputes and largely through the fear of another national strike, Prime Minister David Lloyd George approved a Royal Commission of Inquiry – under the High Court Judge Sir John Sankey – to investigate all aspects of the industry. The Commission's interim report, which included a backdated wage award, was accepted by parliament and strike action was called off; but the second-stage options, in particular the public ownership (nationalisation) of the mines was rejected by the Lloyd George government in favour of a much more modest 'state-sponsoring' scheme.

Timeline of coal mine disaster fatalities (5+), 1910-1919

19 January 1910: **Hattonrigg**, Lanarkshire: (winding)	8
7 May 1910: **Water Haigh**, Leeds, Yorkshire: (sinking)	6
11 May 1910: **Wellington**, Whitehaven, Cumberland: (explosion/fire)	136
21 December 1910: **Pretoria,** Atherton, Lancashire: (explosion)	344
25 November 1911: **Bignall Hill**, Audley, Staffordshire: (explosion)	6
14 December 1911: **Hednesford**, Hednesford, Staffordshire: (explosion)	5
18 May 1912: **Markham**, Blackwood, Monmouthshire: (explosion)	6
9 July 1912: **Cadeby Main**, Doncaster, Yorkshire: (explosions)	88 (91)
7 February 1913: **Rufford**, Mansfield, Nottinghamshire: (sinking)	14
6 June 1913: **Car House**, Rotherham, Yorkshire: (inrush)	8
3 August 1913: **Cadder No 15**, Lanarkshire: (fire)	22
14 October 1913: **Universal**, Senghenydd, Glamorganshire: (explosion)	440
18 October 1913: **Glynea**, Bynea, Carmarthenshire: (explosion)	8
30 May 1914: **Wharncliffe Silkstone**, Barnsley, Yorkshire: (explosion)	11
17 January 1915: **Podmore Hall (Minnie)**, Halmer End, Staffordshire: (explosion)	9
25 February 1915: **New Hem Heath,** Chesterton, Staffordshire: (fire)	12
26 April 1915: **Brayton Domain**, Cumberland: (explosion)	7
30 June 1915: **Bentinck**, Kirkby in Ashfield, Nottinghamshire: (winding)	10
21 September 1915: **Exhall**, Nuneaton, Staffordshire: (fire)	14
22 October 1915: **Pennant Hill**, Dudley, Staffordshire: (explosion)	5
26 April 1916: **Neilsland**, Lanarkshire: (inrush)	5
13 August 1916: **Woodhorn**, Ashington, Northumberland: (explosion)	13
11 December 1917: **Crontin**, Widnes, Lancashire: (explosion)	8
12 January 1918: **Podmore Hall (Minnie)**, Halmer End, Staffordshire: (explosion)	156
9 July 1918: **Stanrigg**, Airdre, Lanarkshire: (inrush)	19
6 April 1919: **Oxcroft**, Creswell, Derbyshire: (explosion)	6

Wellington

The night of Wednesday, 11 May 1910 was the start of a terrible and long-lasting period of distress for the families associated with miners who were at work in Wellington Pit, owned by the Whitehaven Colliery Company. Following an ignition of gas and a fire, 136 of the 142 men and boys lost their lives in Cumberland's worst mine disaster. What made the event so tragic was that some of the miners were still alive following the initial explosion, their chalked messages inscribed on doors and pieces of timber. After over 30 hours of attempts at rescue the decision of the regional inspector of mines, J.B. Atkinson, in consultation with the Chief Inspector of Mines (R.A.S. Redmayne) and the Home Secretary (Winston Churchill) to seal off the fire-affected area (and therefore starve it of oxygen) would not have been taken lightly. It was a pretty hopeless situation, several 'rescuers' wearing breathing apparatus unable to locate the men and reach the seat of the fire.

Subsequently, in the House of Commons, a debate about the circumstances of the disaster, included a sharp exchange of views between Churchill and the Merthyr Tydfil MP, Keir Hardie, especially regarding the decision to wall up the main underground routeway. The outcome was that Hardie clarified any of his comments that may have been taken to

This postcard of Wellington Pit, dating from about 1905, has had details of the disaster added to the image by an enterprising photographer or publisher.

attest blame on the inspectors' decision, though he still firmly believed that some of the men were still alive. Basing his argument on his own mining experiences and conversations with working miners, Hardie concluded by saying that 'not a single life need to have been sacrificed' if a 'proper means of escape' had been available other than the roadway in which the fire took place. Understandably, even after 110 years, and despite all the expert evidence, some descendants of those that perished on the night of 11 May 1910, may feel that some of the trapped men and boys were still alive when the pit was sealed. Sadly, we will never know.

Among the events to mark the centenary of the 1910 Wellington pit disaster was the unveiling of a new monument by the South Beach in Whitehaven in memory of the 136 men and boys who lost their lives. A gold-lettered inscription also records the fact that 64 Edward Medals were awarded 'for the heroism in attempting to rescue the trapped miners'. This was an extraordinary record of gallantry, by far the most number of medals awarded for one event in the history of British mining. One recipient, John Thorne, had already recently received a First Class (silver) Edward Medal for his bravery at the Hamstead disaster of 1908, so was awarded a bar to his award. This was a very exceptional occurrence. Only two bars were ever awarded, the other to George Handle Silkstone, an enginewright, for his bravery at Water Haigh pit, also in 1910 (on 7 May and 17 November). The bravery of another rescuer, James Littlewood, was also deemed to be so outstanding that he also got a First Class medal. Wearing Meco breathing apparatus, Thorne and Littlewood, from Sheffield, had advanced towards the fire, through black smoke, deadly fumes and heat so intense that their helmet metal name plates had melted; and their legs were scorched, before with great reluctance they had to abandon their search.

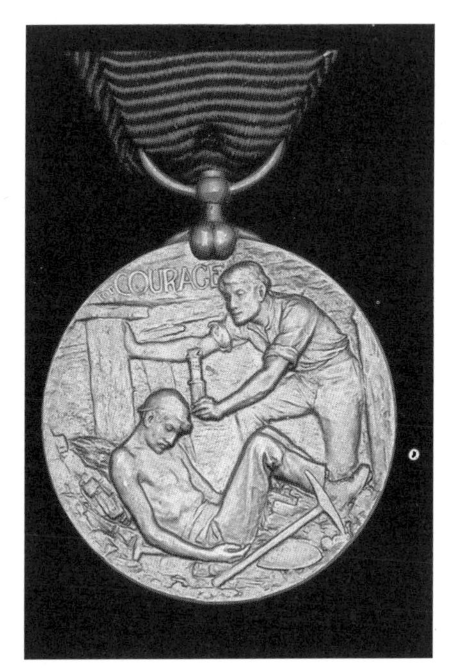

The new memorial and an Edward Medal.

To raise cash for the disaster fund, the Whitehaven printers W.H.Halton and Sons produced a large (15 × 10 inches) booklet containing a full list of the 'men who were entombed' and (most of) their portraits, priced at 6d (2.5p). The photographs appear to have been obtained from studio, wedding, military and sporting images, cleverly assembled in montages by a local man, J. Leech. Left to right they are (top row:) G.Ritson (senr), James Taylor, Ed McAllister, John Joyce and Tom Brannon; (middle row:) Geo Boyd, Tom McAllister, John Anderson, Tom Joyce and Jacob Glaister; (bottom row:) John McAllister; Joseph McQuilliam, William Bell, J.H. Walker and Daniel Branch. Of the above, the McAllisters lost seven family members and three Brannon brothers died in the disaster.

Pretoria (Hulton)

Barely a month after the enquiry into the Wellington Colliery disaster was completed, on 21 December 1910, the Pretoria Colliery at Westhoughton, near Atherton in Lancashire (owned by the Hulton Company) exploded with such violence at about 8 am that 344 men and boys were to lose their lives. It remains England's worst pit disaster as a result of a single devastating event and is the third most serious in British mining history.

Thought to have been caused by a gas build-up, ignited by a faulty lamp, Joseph Shearer Staveley, aged 16, an apprentice fitter, one of the few survivors of a part of the pit known as the Yard Mine (coal seam), quoted in *The Times* newspaper on December 23, 1910, had this to say:

> 'We had just got into the pump house when the explosion took place. It sounded like a cannon going off. It knocked me to the ground, but the fitter kept his feet. We made our way along the Arley Pit, when the fitter fell, and I fell over him. We had felt the gas very strongly. I lay there, I think, for about an hour. When I woke up I found the fitter was dead. I made my wife up to the Arley Pit and shouted for about an hour. About ten o'clock a [rescue] party came down. I saw nobody else alive in the Yard Mine, and I did not think that I should be saved.'

James Staveley is shown at the centre of this postcard 'celebrating' three of the 'only' survivors of the Pretoria pit disaster. Staveley was one of four persons found alive in the Yard Mine of the No.3 Pit on the first day; and one of two that survived (the other being Alfred Davenport, aged 20). John Sharples was taken to hospital suffering from gas inhalation but recovered. Some 545 miners actually got out of the pit, but from the No.4 Pit. As at other disasters, some 'featured' survivors deemed to be so 'lucky' assumed legendary status, at least locally, for years to come.

In the neighbouring communities that 'served' the Pretoria Colliery, few families were not affected by the aftermath of the disaster. *The Times* reporter noted that 'every other house at Chequerbent and Wingates had its blinds drawn today, and few families have escaped losing one or more members. A Wingates family has lost the father and five sons. The last case has a peculiar pathos, as the youngest son was making his first descent into the mine.'

The many funerals were described in great detail in the local and regional press. The words of the Rector of the Sacred Heart church was typical:

> 'No-one will ever forget the sights...the hearses, the mourning coaches, the long funeral processions, the throngs of grieving widows and orphans, relatives and friends, the hundreds of visitors, all of them making their way to the last resting places. To see the people in tears, to hear the sobbing and sighing of the wives and children, brothers and sisters, was something beyond human endurance.'

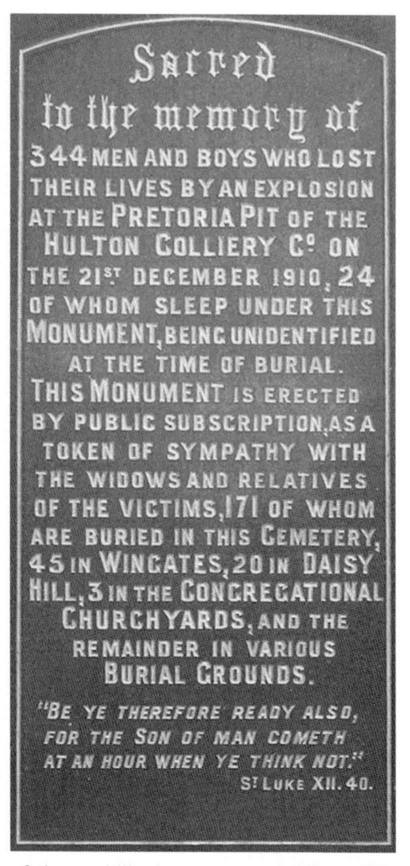

The 'Pretoria' cenotaph in Westhoughton cemetery. Almost two-thirds of those killed were aged 13 to 30; and the main cause of death for the majority, again almost two-thirds, was carbon monoxide poisoning. A detailed account of the disaster can be found via the Parish of Westhoughton's website: www.lan-opc.org.uk/westhoughton/ pretoria/index.html. For their extraordinary bravery at Hulton Colliery ten miners were awarded the Edward Medal.

Cadeby Main

Few pit disasters have attracted such media attention, regionally, nationally and internationally as the terrible events on 9 July 1912 at Cadeby Main colliery, Denaby Main near Doncaster. A royal visit to the locality by King George V and Queen Mary had resulted in an unusually low number of miners at work during the night shift, when at about 1.30 am, an explosion ripped through the South District of the mine. The 'royal connection' zoomed to prominence in many of the subsequent press reports. Thirty-five 'mature' Cadeby miners aged between 18 and 67 were killed, mostly from 'burns'. During the mid-morning rescue operations a second explosion resulted in an even greater loss of life: fifty-three more fatalities, including the senior HM inspector of mines, Henry Richardson Hewitt and the Divisional Inspector of Mines, William Henry Pickering (also his young assistant, Gilbert Young Tickle). For his bravery, Pickering had been awarded the Edward medal (first class) at the Water Haigh disaster in Yorkshire just two years earlier. The courage of six individuals involved in the search and rescue at Cadeby were subsequently presented with Edward medals, two deputies (George Fisher abd Harry Halley) getting first class awards.

There were three 'unofficial' fatalities: a related suicide (Frank Wood); a rescue team man (James Burns) who died from poisonous gas inhalation over a month later; and the death, eight months after the disaster date, of a deputy (James Springthorpe) who survived the first explosion.

Women and nurses (some with bicycles) appear in the foreground of this postcard image (one of several published after the disaster); and a horse-and trap makes its way through part of a great crowd of mostly flat-capped men 'waiting for news' in the shadow of Cadeby Main.

Souvenir in Affectionate Remembrance of the

Miners' and the Rescue Party

WHO LOST THEIR LIVES IN THE

CADEBY MAIN COLLIERY, YORKSHIRE,

JULY 9th, 1912.

About 7 p.m, the King and Queen drove up in a motor-car. Most of the watchers had gone home. An almost imperceptible murmur went around that the King and Queen had come. The crowd closed round the motor. 2 police officers, almost as surprised as the people pulled smartly to attention, but there was no attempt to keep back the crowd. All was informal everything completely natural. Little children clustered round, and with wondering eyes looked up into the face of the King and Queen. The King wore an

expression of deep concern as though some very personal calamity had occured

Tears glisten in the eyes of the Queen as she hurried up the steps anxious to learn the fullest details The Queen emerged with bowed head tears still filled her eyes, and she gazed across the valley to the pithead. A Queen was in tears with a grief that was as real as that of those around. The cheer of the little group, whose loyalty outweighed even their grief, died away into a sob.

THE KING and QUEEN'S MESSAGES.

Their Majesties are shocked to hear of the terrible accident at your Colliery The fact that their Majestics were near to the scene in the midst of so much rejoicing when visiting Wendover yesterday brings home to them still more the sorrow and sadness which now prevails amongst you. I desire to express their Majesties' heartfelt sympathy with the families of those who have perished and with the sufferers in this grievous calamity. *STAMFORDHAM.*

Their Majesties' have visited the Cadeby Colliery to-day to ascertain personally particulars of the sad calamity which has deprived so many of us of those we love. They command me to express to all who have suffered the lost of any who are dear to them their deep sympathy with them in their grief.

LIST OF MINERS and RESCUE PARTY.

Fred Richardson
J W Thompson
W Franklin
G Denton
P Evans
T Walsh
G Alderson
C Hunt
T Burns
M Jordan
C Fletcher
J Boycott
M Mulrooney
G W Hudson
A Dungworth
J Marsden
Roodhouse
Gasooigne

P E Nicholson
J McDonagh
J Smith
E Henderson
C Rodgers
T Coady
J Mulhorn
C Radley
H Thompson
W Green
W H Pickering
H R Hewitt,
C Y Tickle
Douglas Chambers
J Springthorpe
W Somerscales
R W Chapman
R P Bungard

B Ward
J Carlton
R Neal Edington
F Walton
S Webster
R Winpenny
J Philipps
F Horsfall
J Turner
W Davis
J Fox
G Whitton
W Wallace
J Shuttleworth
C Treffrey
T Stribley
W Ackroyd
Chas Bury

H McGarnett
T Talbert
J Kelsall
J Tarbrook
W Waters
J Burdiken
T Fleck
H Neal
T Hancock
W Lambert
J Ross
M Hayden
A Flynn
E Tuffy
Mr Cusworth
C Prince
C Heptinstall

Printer S Burgess 8 York Place, Strand, London W.C.

Detail of a souvenir napkin/serviette printed on tissue paper by S.Burgess of The Strand, London to commemorate the Cadeby Main disaster of 1912. Though very delicate, it is a remarkable testimony to the care of local families that a few of these have survived intact, in private collections and museums.

Generations of people – including descendants of some of those who lost their lives – attended a parade and service of remembrance at Denaby Main to mark the centenary of the Cadeby Main disaster in 2012; and for the unveiling of a new memorial in the cemetery, the culmination of a great deal of research and fund raising by the Cadeby Main Memorial Group.

Senghenydd (Universal Colliery)

The enormity of the 'Senghenydd' disaster – the deaths of 440 men and boy miners (including William John who died during rescue attempts) – has affected thousands of lives right up to the present day. Undoubtedly the most astonishing and annoying feature of the worst disaster in British coalmining history was that the Universal Colliery Company, in its greed for profit, had blatantly ignored safety legislation in the new (1911) Coal Mines Act. A fine of only £24 was imposed on the manager whilst the owners got away with 'compensation' of just £10 and £5.5s.0d in costs following legal challenges in the courts.

The Universal Colliery closed in 1928 and the remaining surface features were cleared in 1963. A memorial in the form of a scaled-down headgear was placed near to the site, close to Nant-y-Parc primary school, in 1981. The new (1913) Welsh National and Universal Memorial Garden was created to commemorate the disasters at the colliery and in Wales as a whole. Like the excellent Aber Valley Heritage Museum (www.thecentresenghenydd.co.uk CF83 4HA) in Senghenydd, it is well worth visiting.

Right: This postcard image, one of a remarkable series produced by the photographer W. Benton of Glasgow, shows Keir Hardie (centre) alongside one of the colliery's directors (on the left) and a local miners' union man.

Two typical postcard images (above and below) from the camera of W. Benton help us to appreciate the crowded scene at the pit head of the Universal Colliery following the explosion on 14 October 1913. It is remarkable how close onlookers were able to assemble, whilst police, rescuers and a variety of 'officials' did what they could to assist. By July 1914 the appeal fund in support of over 800 dependants (widows, children and dependent mothers and fathers) had reached £126,000 (about £8 million in today's money). But nothing could really compensate for the loss of one or more family members.

'Waiting for News' is a life-size carving by the tree surgeon and sculptor Dai Edwards, forming part of the new Miners' Memorial Garden at Senghenydd. It represents a 13-year-old girl (Agnes May Webber) nursing her baby sister, Gwyneth and is based on one of W. Benton's photographs. In the background some of the former miners' houses can be seen. The sculpture was sponsored by CISWO (Coal Industry Social Welfare Organisation).

Minnie Pit (Podmore Hall Colliery)

When Podmore Hall colliery's Minnie Pit 'fired' on 12 January 1918, at a time that the Great War was still raging, the outcome was extraordinarily tragic: 155 miners and Hugh Doorbar, the captain of the Birchenwood Colliery (No.1) rescue team were killed; and about a third of all the fatalities were 'boy-miners', teenagers with so much life ahead of them.

Podmore miner Frank Halfpenny's gallantry was such during the aftermath of the disaster that he was awarded the Edward Medal (First Class).

The impact of the disaster on Halmerend and its neighbouring pit villages was massive, with close-knit communities already affected by losses of loved ones during the war. Despite what could be done by the miners' union and contributions from a public relief fund, many families were reduced to a subsistence existence alongside their great personal distress.

Ian Bailey, from the Audley and District Family History Society, by the side of one of the contemporary memorials to the Minnie Pit disaster, in 2013, part of an appeal for 'memories and information' in preparation for a new publication by the Society to be published to commemorate the centenary of the disaster in 2018.

A 24-year-old soldier of the 3rd/5th battalion of Manchester regiment, in barracks near the North Yorkshire seaside town of Scarborough in January 1918, a few weeks after treatment recuperation at Craiglockhart War Hospital in Edinburgh, was so emotionally affected by the Minnie Pit disaster (and no doubt its associations with his recent shocking experiences on the Western Front) that he expressed his feelings in a poem. His name was Wilfred Owen, later to become one of the most famous poetic voices of the Great War. *The Miners*, apparently written 'in half an hour', was Owen's first poem to appear in print nationally – in *The Nation* – and one of only a handful of his poems published in his own lifetime. Returning to active service, Owen was killed in action on 4 November 1918, a week before the signing of the Armistace.

Wilfred Owen (1893-1918). (Public domain: from *Poems of Wilfred Owen*, 1920).

The Miners includes the following lines, so relevant to the disaster:

> *But the coals were murmuring of their mine,*
> *And moans down there*
> *Of boys that slept wry sleep, and men*
> *Writhing for air.*

As does the concluding verse:

> *The centuries will burn rich loads*
> *With which we groaned,*
> *Whose warmth shall lull their dreaming lids,*
> *While songs are crooned;*
> *But they will not dream of us poor lads,*
> *Left in the ground.*

Chapter Three

1920-1929
'... the sad bells of Rhymney'

(From *Gwalia Deserta* ['Wasteland of Wales'], Part XV, Idris Davis, 1938)

Mining continued to be a highly dangerous occupation in the immediate post-war years. In his evidence to the Samuel Commission (1925-26), the miners' leader Herbert Smith made the point that for every work day more than five miners were killed. Furthermore, for every 100 men working in the industry for twenty years, two would be killed, nine would suffer serious injury, sixteen experience debilitating disease, and each man would be off work for seven or more days following some kind of accident. Excluding the national strike years of 1921 and 1926 (and a small fall in fatalities in 1928), the annual number of men and boys loosing their lives in mining accidents remained well over a thousand a year, peaking at an horrendous 1,297 in 1923.

Unfortunately, for politicians, mine owners (the pits were now back in private control) and the general public, it was the disasters and their associated media coverage that engendered any 'acknowledgement' of the need for reform. In 1920, the establishment of the Safety in Mines Research Board under the chair of His Majesty's Chief Inspector of Mines was a step in the right direction, as was the first nationwide 'Safety First' campaign launched two years later; and also the new 'experimental research' stations at Eskmeals (Cumberland) and then Harpur Hill (Buxton, Derbyshire). But much more needed to be done in order to at least ameliorate the dangers of mining coal by people and, increasingly, by machinery. However, two health-related innovations were welcomed by the miners: the appointment of the first Medical Inspector of Mines and the introduction of pithead baths.

Ironically, the 'good news' was that the number of 5-plus-fatality disasters had reduced slightly compared with the previous decade; and, much more significantly, there were no what might be called 'mega disasters' of the kind that had so recently devastated so many communities in South Wales, Cumberland, Lancashire, Staffordshire and Yorkshire. That said, the still major disasters at Haig (Cumberland, 39 dead), Marine (South Wales: 52) and Maltby Main (Yorkshire: 27) were each a consequence of explosions (and their associated aftermaths); and inrushes of water continued to account for many fatalities, most notably in old mining areas at Redding (Scotland: 40) and Montagu (Northumberland: 38). Like giant exclamation marks, the disasters really did draw attention to a much a wider 'safety-at-work' problem in the coalmining industry of Britain after the First World War.

By 1929 unemployment in the mining industry had reached crisis levels, and many of those miners still working were reduced to two and three shifts a week. Around a quarter of a million men and boy miners were 'on the dole', about the same number that had followed Kitchener's call to arms a decade or so earlier. 'Manpower' in the coalmining industry had fallen below a million for the first time in twenty years, the start of a long and steady decline in employment. The 'wicked thirties', exceptionally bad years of great poverty and distress in so many coalfield communities, was yet to come.

Timeline of coal mine disaster fatalities (5+), 1920-1929

Disaster	Fatalities
13 July 1922: **East Plean**, Bannockburn, Stirlingshire: (explosion)	12
5 September 1922: **Haig Pit**, Whitehaven, Cumberland: (explosion)	39
27 November 1922: **St Helen's** (Siddick), Workington, Cumberland: (explosion)	6
22 February 1923: **Whedale**, Castleford, Yorkshire: (explosion)	9
24 February 1923: **Medomsley (Busty Pit)**, Consett, Durham: (winding)	8
26 April 1923: **Trimsaran**, Pembrey, Carmarthen: (transport/haulage)	10
28 July 1923: **Gartshore**, Dunbartonshire: (explosion)	8
28 July 1923: **Maltby Main**, Rotherham, Yorkshire: (explosion):	27
25 September 1923: **Redding**, Falkirk, Stirlingshire: (inrush):	40
3 December 1923: **Nunnery**, Sheffield, Yorkshire: (haulage):	7
3 September 1924: **Ponthenry**, Llanelly, Glamorganshire: (gas outburst)	5
27 November 1924: **Killan**, Dunvant, Glamorganshire: (inrush)	5
5 December 1924: **Llay Main**, Wrexham, Denbighshire: (explosion)	9
30 March 1925: **Montagu**, Scotswood, Northumberland: (inrush)	38
9 August 1925: **Wallsend** (Edward Pit), Northumberland : (explosion)	5
4 November 1925: **Pendleton**, Lancashire: (upheaval/gas/explosion)	6
18 December 1925: **Birchenwood**, Kidsgrove, Staffordshire: (explosion)	7
15 March 1926: **Thorne**, Doncaster, Yorkshire: (sinking)	6
1 March 1927: **Bilsthorpe**, Nottinghamshire: (sinking)	14
1 March 1927: **Marine**, Cwm, Ebbw Vale : (explosion)	52
12 February 1928: **Haig Pit**, Whitehaven, Cumberland: (explosion)	13
18 March 1929: **Coombs Wood**, Halesowen, Worcestershire: (fire)	8
10 July 1929: **Milfraen**, Blaenavon, Monmouthshire: (explosion)	9
28 November 1929: **Wernbwll**, Penclawdd, Glamorganshire: (explosion)	7

Getting coal from gaseous and fiery anthracite seams, south Wales miners continued to experience inexcusably hazardous working conditions. Some areas were so dangerous that they should never have been worked. This was the case at Ponthenry Colliery near Llanelly, where the Pumpquart part of its drift mines was noted for sudden emissions or 'blowers' of gas, resulting in several fatalities. The most serious event was when five men died 'due to suffocation' (asphyxia) following a sudden outburst of gas whilst working the 'soft coal' in the Glynhir Slant, on 3 September 1925. The deceased were William Henry Evans (married, nine children); William David Jenkins (married, five children); Samuel Evans (married, four children); George Buck and Stanley Morris. Eight miners involved in the rescue operations were subsequently honoured with Carnegie certificates in recognition of their bravery.

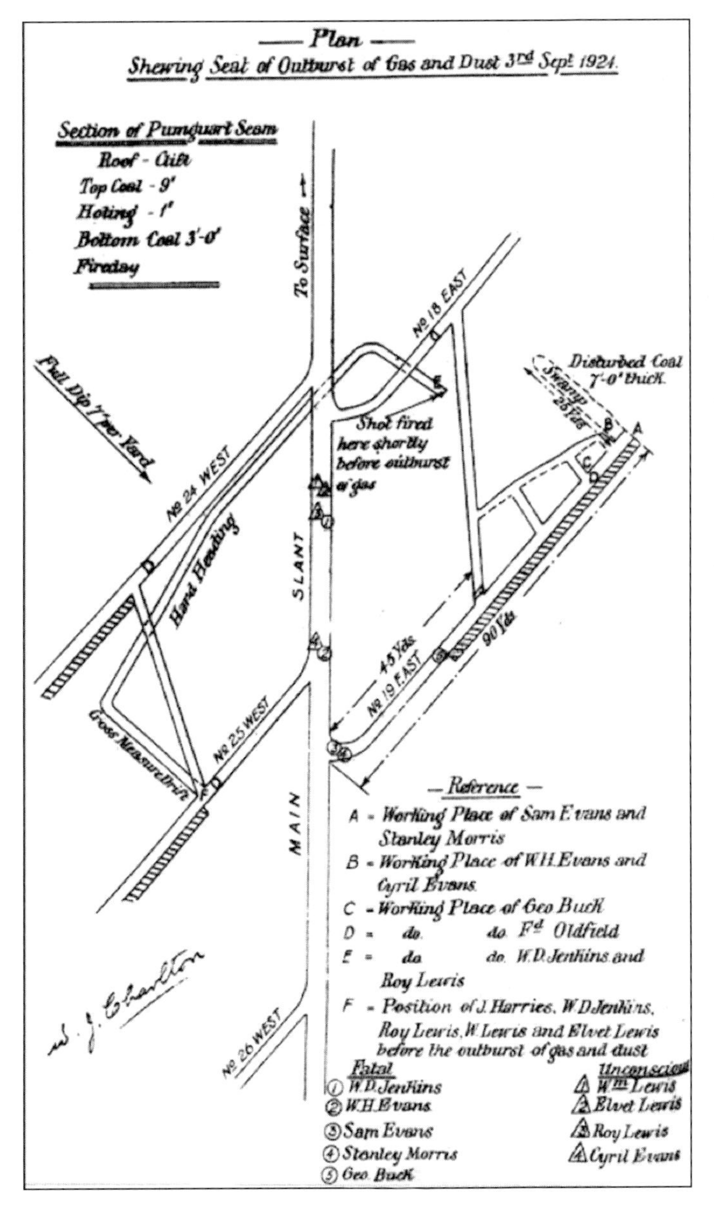

This detailed plan of the workings where the disaster occurred was issued to the inquest by the Ponthenry Colliery's manager, George Joblings. Less than four years later two more miners were killed in the same mine in similar circumstances. Ponthenry continued to work until 1936.

With the very best of intentions, when a pair of miners fired three shots to adjust the coalface in the Montagu View pit in Scotswood, near Newcastle, on the morning of 30 March 1925 the outcome proved to be devastating for many of their mates. Soon, millions of gallons of water rushed through the mine, fatally trapping thirty-eight miners. This was despite tremendous heroics of the rescue teams from Elswick, Houghton and Ashington; and a local brigade headed by the pit manager, G. Nicholson. What the terrible conditions above and below ground was like is impossible to visualize, though the final sequences of Carol Reed's film (page 54) provide a realistic impression of events.

Families taking refreshment whilst waiting for news following the Montagu pit disaster. Scotswood village was badly affected, twenty-two of the deceased residing there. Such was the volume of water and foul-air conditions, it took months for the last bodies to be recovered, the identification impossible in some cases.

Rain pours down on the waiting crowd at Montagu View Colliery following the 'inrush of water' disaster there, on 30 March 1925. The mass funerals at Elswick cemetery of those miners whose bodies were retrieved were also accompanied by heavy downpours of rain, the tragic aftermath placed in verse by a local miner-poet, Sid Smith:

'For it was in a flooded mine their lives they gave,
Interred to the sodden earth half-filled watery grave,
And as the rain clouds banked slowly to the West,
Those miners of Tyneside were at last laid to rest'.

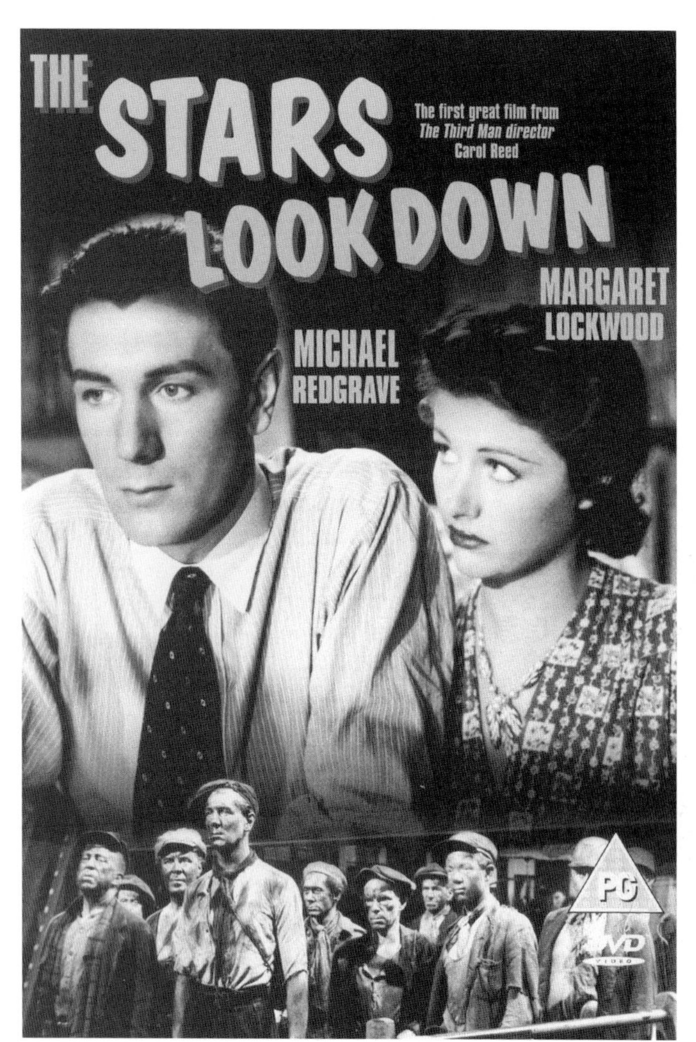

The Montagu disaster is believed to have inspired part of one of the most famous novels of A.J. Cronin, *The Stars Look Down* (1935), subsequently adapted and released in 1940 as a film of the same name, starring Michael Redgrave and Margaret Lockwood (and directed by Carol Reed). The realistic film scenes were actually shot in Cumberland. In 1975 the playwright Alan Plater made a further adaption of Cronin's novel for a television series. Now available as a DVD, the colliery-based footages are well worth seeing today.

At about 5am on Tuesday 25 September 1923 a great inrush of water from disused workings flooded Number 23 pit at Redding Colliery, near Falkirk, trapping sixty-six men. Within a day rescue teams had got out twenty-one miners, still alive. Hope of finding more men was never totally abandoned in the ensuing few days, despite the presence of 'black-damp', the deadly 'after-mixture' of gas that permeated the underground workings and roadways, well-known and feared by generations of miners. In one of the most astonishing rescues in British mining history, five of the trapped men were found alive *after nine days* and conveyed to the surface. It wasn't until December that the remaining forty bodies were recovered, the courageous searchers wearing diving gear and breathing apparatus. Extant in Falkirk Archives are pencilled notes on torn-out pages from a Time Book, probably written in almost complete darkness during his entrapment by Thomas Thomson, to his wife Elizabeth and children Willie and Jean. From his jottings it appears that Thomson was left alive after at least eight days, but sadly he was not found, his body recovered on 7 November 1923, the poignant notes found in his 'piece box (lunch tin)'.

James Jack pictured with his children. Jack and his four mates had survived an incredible nine days underground without food.

'A NINE-DAYS WONDER:' This artist's impression of the rescue party breaking through the barrier of fallen rock debris, an arm and hand of one of the trapped men reaching towards them, probably captures the dramatic underground scene at Redding more graphically than any photographic image could. It was the work of A. Forester 'artist at the Redding Pit', based on details given to him by the rescuers. The outstretched arm belonged to Andrew Thomson, senior. The five men had spent all the time huddled together, keeping their sprits up by stories and jokes, some relating to their Great War experiences.

Inset: Andrew Thomson, back home with his wife.

ERECTED TO THE MEMORY OF
THE FORTY MEN WHO LOST THEIR LIVES
IN THE DISASTER AT REDDING COLLIERY
TUESDAY 25TH SEPTEMBER 1923.

THOMAS BROWN	THOMAS BROWN (2)	ARCHIBALD McNEE
JOHN FORRESTER	JAMES LENNIE WRIGHT	DAVID BENNIE
DAVID PORTEOUS	THOMAS THOMSON	ROBERT THOMSON
FRANK McGARVIE	JAMES MARRS	ANDREW BROWN
MICHAEL McKENNA	LAWRENCE T. SCOBBIE	HENRY THOMSON
ANDREW ANDERSON	DAVID THOMSON	ROBERT BEVERIDGE
WILLIAM ANDERSON	JAMES SCOTT IRVING	JOHN BEEKMAN
PATRICK SHIELDS	ALEX. HAMILTON	THOMAS THOMSON (2)
JAMES HANNAN	LAWRENCE THOMSON	JAMES ADAM
THOMAS AITKEN	WILLIAM DONALDSON	COLIN MAXWELL, JNR.
THOMAS THOMSON, JNR.	COLIN MAXWELL	MICHAEL McLAUGHLIN
THOMAS KILGANNAN	THOMAS BONAR	JAMES JARVIE
DAVID BROWN	JOHN BAXTER	JAMES COCHRANE
	WALTER MAXWELL	

RESCUED ALIVE AFTER TEN DAYS ENTOMBED
JOHN DONALDSON JAMES JACK JOHN MILLER ROBERT URE ANDREW THOMSON
THEIR NAMES LIVE ON FOR EVERMORE

The plaque on the memorial to the Redding disaster lists all the men who died as well as the five miners 'rescued alive after ten days entombed'. Placed on a stone plinth, it was unveiled in 1980 at Redding Cross by Mrs William Easton who lost her father, brother and uncle in the disaster. The pit was closed by the NCB in 1958. Laurence Thomson, rescued from the pit via the gutterhole on the first day of the disaster, is believed to have been the 'last survivor', passing away in April 1986. Redding and other 'inrushes' led to the establishment of a procedure for abandoned mine plans to be lodged and consulted by managers and engineers when exploring and developing new working areas. The disasters also pointed to the importance of an accurate record being kept of who was down a mine at any particular time, a requirement not made fully legal until 1956.

Veteran Free Collier Robert Jack, grandson of James Jack, one of the five rescued trapped miners, lays a wreath at the Redding disaster memorial in 2013, on the 90th anniversary of the disaster. A Great war hero, James Jack died suddenly aged 44 in 1930.

On the morning of 28 July 1923 a new shift of volunteer pitmen at Maltby Main near Rotherham, in south Yorkshire were trying to combat dangerous 'gob' (waste) fires, which had been affecting work and production for several months, when a huge explosion occurred following a build up of methane gas. Twenty-seven of the miners were killed, the violence of the blast so great that only one body, that of Original Renshaw, was recovered.

Local communities continue to commemorate mining disasters by commissioning new memorials in honour of those who died. The ceremonies provide a new annual focus for future generations and remind us of the heavy price that was paid by the miners and their families in order to keep pit faces and mines working. Perhaps nowhere was a new commemoration more important than at Maltby on 28 July 2015, when a granite memorial stone engraved with the names of the twenty-seven miners who had died in the disaster at Maltby Main in 1923 was unveiled on the outskirts of the village, along Lime Kiln Lane, above the underground spot where the disaster had occurred ninety-two years earlier.

Rescue brigades and ambulance crews from surrounding pits rushed to aid the Maltby rescue team on 28 July 1923, and did what they could until all hope of finding any man alive was abandoned by late afternoon. The only agreed and safe option was to seal off the affected area by the erection of substantial 'stoppings' (barriers of brick or stone) in the main roadways. The Maltby Main Colliery rescue team are shown here displaying a variety of what was then 'state of the art' equipment at St Anne's rescue station, Rotherham; but note the caged canary on the left of the image, ever-present at many mines right through to the 1980s.

Many years after the Maltby disaster, on 14 November 1947, the unidentified remains of another of the men was found when sealed-off workings were accessed. After a well-attended funeral the miner was laid to rest in Grange Lane cemetery, his grave, located to the left of the main entrance, is shown in the foreground, laid flat. The memorial stone, erected by the Maltby miners and National Coal Board, has a concluding inscription at its base: THEY THAT DIED BROUGHT US LIGHT/THEY THAT LIVE BRING US FELLOWSHIP.

The most serious accident during the 1920s took place in south Wales at the Ebbw Vale Company's Marine Colliery on 1 March (St David's Day) 1927. Fifty-two men and boys lost their lives following an explosion in the Black Vein seam area and the small mining village of Cwm that served the pit was devastated by the event. It was also the worst Welsh disaster since the Senghenydd tragedy of 1913. This rare press image, issued for American usage, shows members of the rescue team wearing Proto breathing equipment, leaving the pithead, understandably grim-faced, their role 'reduced' to the recovery of bodies.

Prime Minister Stanley Baldwin, who with his wife had been at a St David's Day event in Cardiff, was motored to the Marine Colliery to pay his respects. Lining the PM's route to the pit office, some very agitated miners targeted their feelings towards Baldwin, telling him to 'go down...and get those boys out of the Black Vein' and bemoaned the newly-imposed 8-hour day. The Baldwin entourage also called at the house of William Button (22 Canning Street, Cwm) whose elder son, Bert, having arrived safely at the pit bottom, had gone back to the area of the explosion in search of his younger brother Wilfred, and so lost his own life. Two sons lost. The 'demonstration' against Baldwin was said to be 'resented in the district' and 'condemned by several of the leaders of the Labour Party'.

The creative works of the Rhymney-born poet and schoolteacher Idris Davis (1905-1953) was much affected by the disaster at Cwm; as well as the economic and social distress that permeated local communities during and in the wake of the 1921 miners' strike and the long 1926 lock-out. As a teenager and young man Davis had spent his formative years working in McLaren and Maerdy pits; and had himself experienced an accident underground, losing his little finger, prior to Maerdy closing, a blessing perhaps as it enabled him to begin the 'self-study' that let him access further and higher education. Idris never forgot his roots, his first major work, *Gwalia deserta* (1938) reflecting the parlous state of industrial south Wales in the inter-war years. Set to music and most notably performed by the folk singer Peter Seeger, *The Bells of Rhymney,* from the 'Deserta' volume, has become one of Davis's most well-known poems; and one of the best ever written that relates to a twentieth-century mining disaster.

Ambulance 'competitions' and their leagues were extremely important incentives for the training and continued competency of 'first-aiders' at collieries. This silver medal was presented to H.C. Harris, a member of the Tirpentwys senior team in 1923, part of the Southern Mines Inspection District's ambulance league. Near Pontypool, Tirpentwys Colliery employed over 1,600 men and boys in 1923, steam and house coal extracted from several seams, including Black Vein. Tirpentwys was the scene of a serious winding accident in 1902 when eight lives were lost. The pit closed in 1969.

The Whitehaven area of the Cumberland coalfield continued to experience serious accidents during the post-1918 period, most notably at Haig Pit. The explosion there on 5 September 1922 resulted in thirty-nine young miners, mostly aged between 19 and 30, losing their lives following an explosion. Those killed included George McCreadie and his two sons, Robert and Gordon, from the badly affected Thwaiteville (ex-army) huts at Kells. The blast was so severe that numerous roof falls hindered the searchers; and the impact of the 'afterdamp' on the underground air circulation was so bad that it took until 10 September for all the bodies to be recovered. The cause of the explosion was believed to have been the firing of a shot which ignited 'firedamp', the blast aided by the presence of coal dust, according to the official report submitted by Thomas Mottram, HM Chief Inspector of Mines. Mottram also concluded that 12-hour consecutive shifts, worked by a key deputy, was both inappropriate and unsafe for his duties to be carried out properly.

The caption on this Haig Pit postcard was probably added after the 1922 disaster, produced by Benton of Hull.

Carrying a caged canary in one hand and oil lamp in the other – but wearing no safety apparatus – this young unnamed miner appeared in the national (*The Times*) and local press as 'a member of a rescue party...going to join another gallant attempt to reach the doomed men', after the 1922 Haig Pit disaster.

A few years later, on 13 December 1927, Haig Pit was 'in the news' again, four men losing their lives following an explosion about the time that the night shift was due to start. Such were the air conditions, one of the bodies, that of Harold Horrocks, had to be abandoned. Then on 12 February 1928, during efforts to re-open stoppings in order to restore working opportunities, further explosions took place resulting in the deaths of another thirteen men. The fatalities consisted principally of experienced officials – deputies and overman – and the blasts also cost the lives of two junior mines inspectors, a Miners' Association agent, the colliery's under-manager and the works manager Robert Steel. The experienced Steel had won the Edward medal in the Wellington pit disaster of 1910 and had participated in the rescues at William Pit in 1907 and 1922. Two of the deputies killed in the December explosion were also veteran rescue men of the Wellington disaster. All thirteen, plus the body of Horrocks, were never recovered.

Responsible people and organisations with interests in the coal industry continued to be perplexed and concerned at the number of incidents and tragic events that took place during the sinking of new collieries and in winding operations: accidents involving 'cages' or 'hoppits' (iron sinkers' buckets) hauled up and down shafts. The most serious of these that took place in the 1920s occurred at Bilsthorpe Colliery, in north Nottinghamshire, on 1 March 1927, the same day of the Marine Colliery disaster in South Wales. Sinkers at Bilsthorpe were working in very difficult conditions, having to combat inflows of water into the developing shaft. The new practice adopted here was to line the shaft with concrete and inject cement into the adjacent strata; but such was the water problem at Bilsthorpe that heavy-duty motor-driven pumps had to be employed and placed at the surface, by the headgear. Unfortunately the 'rising main' (pump pipe) and apparatus crashed to the bottom on top of a hoppit. Remarkably, three men who had been working in the shaft were found alive and eventually rescued, but the thirteen others in and around the hoppit had no chance of survival, either killed under the massive impact of the fallen debris or horrifically drowned as water filled the shaft bottom. It took two weeks for the last of the bodies to be recovered.

A small granite memorial dedicated to the thirteen 'sinkers' who lost their lives in the 'Bilsthorpe disaster' can be seen in St Margaret's churchyard (extension). It was unveiled in 2009.

'Sinkers' were a 'special breed' of pitmen, employed either from a branch of a mining engineering company or a specialist pit-sinker firm. In the 1920s they were often Irish (as were several of the Bilsthorpe fatalities); and before and at the start of the First World War, it was not unusual for groups of German sinkers to be recruited, until internment put paid to this practice. This image – at a north Nottinghamshire pit site – shows a small contingent of sinkers (and local pitmen) wearing their customary oilskins, two of the men standing in a small hoppit (a large iron sinkers' bucket), suspended from a temporary timber headgear, above the shaft, in 1915.

Chapter Four

1930-1939
The 'Wicked' Thirties

The second half of the inter-war period saw no let up in the number and frequency of mining disasters. In fact there were ten more than in the previous decade and the number of 5-plus fatalities had more than doubled, to a total in excess of 800. Taking into consideration day-to-day fatalities, the annual average figure had actually reduced to around 880, though the peak years of 1930 (1013 deaths) and 1934 (1073) were dreadful reminders that much needed to be done for a safer environment for our miners, especially those working underground in potentially hazardous conditions. Almost 8,800 deaths of men and boy miners during the 1930s was a terrible price to pay for the nation's coal supply.

In 1935 the Royal Commission appointed to investigate all aspects of the industry, reported three years later its comments on safety and confirmed that mining continued to be a very dangerous occupation:

> 'If we assume a working life of 50 years, then on average, out of 100 miners entering the industry at 14 years of age, 6.7 will be killed, and around 20 will be seriously injured, the average miner may expect to be injured fairly seriously once in every 5 years during his working life'.

The above facts and comments make even more sober reading in the context of the economic depression that battered the coal industry at this time. Around a quarter of a million miners were unemployed and those in work were invariably reduced to three and four-day weeks. Then in 1931 the McDonald government slashed miners' wages by 10 per cent. Unsurprisingly, the size of the workforce fell by about 100,000 in the 1930s, to well below 800,000. This shrinkage had little to do with mechanisation, which continued to be slow and patchy from coalfield to coalfield.

Poverty widespread, the 'hungry thirties' were, according to one Yorkshire miner, 'wicked' as far as he recalled, with many mine owners taking advantage of the miners' goodwill. It was a situation that began to improve when the outbreak of the Second World War in 1939 focused the nation's attention, yet again, on the strategic importance of Britain's coal supplies.

Disasters continued to attract great public and media interest, increasingly so, because of the development of photography and film. For the first time cinema-goers all over Britain were able to see movie footage of the dreadful pit-top scenes, often focusing on the rescue of the miners as well as the circumstances of the disaster itself.

Although the North East escaped pit disasters, one pit – Hedley Colliery, at South Moor, near Stanley in County Durham – experienced a remarkable event on 29 September 1930, following a roof fall in which a hewer, Fred Beaumont was trapped. Crawling through a narrow and constantly dangerous passageway, teams of miners managed to reach and eventually free Beaumont, after nine hours, the roof collapsing again shortly afterwards. In recognition, the nineteen brave rescuers – each putting his own life in great danger – were awarded the Edward Medal, an exceptional number for the recovery of one man. The 'heroic endeavours' of a further twenty-eight coalminers, pit managers, mines inspectors and medical men were also recognised via Edward medals during the 1930s, four of them receiving the highest, first-class, award.

It was the 'mega' disasters that grabbed public attention most of all, none more so than on a black September day or two at Gresford in north Wales when 266 miners lost their lives in 1934. Major events in Derbyshire, Yorkshire and Nottinghamshire really did demonstrate that the age of the big pit disaster was far from ending; and Scottish pits experienced more disasters during the 1930s than in any other region, culminating at Culross in Fife when an explosion killed thirty-five men at the Valleyfield mine.

The mines inspectors continued to lament that many of the accidents, both singular and multiple-fatality, were 'preventable'. What consolation was that to the bereaved families? Even the smaller multiple-fatality accidents had extraordinary stories of personal misfortunate, almost hidden amid the coroners' inquests, enquiries and media reports. Some smaller disasters were 'forgotten', in the wake of the larger calamities. This may have been the case at Frickley Colliery in Yorkshire in 1931, when five deputies were fatally 'gassed' due to 'gob stink', whilst inspecting the workings after the Christmas holidays. Not long after, nearby Bentley Colliery had exploded resulting in forty-five fatalities in not dissimilar circumstances.

What follows, as with other chapters, are images and commentary regarding a sample of disasters in a single decade. Sadly, more extensive and fuller details would easily fill a book of blockbuster size.

Worst Pit Disaster Since Gresford

79 MINERS DIE IN MARKHAM COLLIERY EXPLOSION

Typical newspaper headline of a 1930s pit disaster: *Sheffield Independent,* 11 May 1938.

Timeline of coal mine disaster fatalities (5+), 1930-1939

24 February 1930: **Wath Main**, Rotherham, Yorkshire: (explosions)	7
26 February 1930: **Lyme Pit**, Haydock, Lancashire: (explosion)	13
10 March 1930: **Allerton Bywater**, Castleford, Yorkshire: (explosion)	5
30 August 1930: **Auchinraith**, Blantyre, Lanarkshire: (explosion)	6
1 October 1930: **Grove Pit**, Brownhills, Staffordshire: (explosion)	14
12 December 1930: **Houghton Main**, Barnsley, Yorkshire: (explosion)	7
22 January 1931: **Auchengeich**, Glasgow, Lanarkshire: (explosion)	6
29 January 1931: **Haig Pit**, Whitehaven, Cumberland: (explosion)	27
3 September 1931: **Newdigate**, Nuneaton, Warwickshire: (explosion)	8
31 October 1931: **Bowhill No.1**, Cardenden, Fifeshire: (explosion)	10
20 November 1931: **Bentley**, Doncaster, Yorkshire: (explosion)	45
28 December 1931: **Frickley**, Pontefract, Yorkshire: (gas)	5
25 January 1932: **Llwynypia**, Porth, Glamorganshire: (explosion)	11
10 October 1932: **Bickershaw**, Leigh, Lancashire: (winding)	19
12 November 1932: **Edge Green (No.9 Pit)**, Ashton, Lancs: explosion:	27
16 November 1932: **Cardowan**, Glasgow, Lanarkshire : (explosion)	11
9 December 1932: **Cortonwood**, Barnsley, Yorkshire :(explosion)	8
16 May 1933: **West Cannock**, Hednesford, Staffordshire: (explosion)	6
19 November 1933: **Grassmore**, Chesterfield, Derbyshire: (explosion)	14
26 July 1934: **Bilsthorpe**, Mansfield, Nottinghamshire: (explosions)	9
14 August 1934: **Rosehall**, Bellshill, Glasgow: (explosion)	5
22 September 1934: **Gresford**, Wrexham, Denbighshire: (explosion/fire)	266
28 August 1935: **South Kirkby**, Yorkshire: (explosion)	10
12 September 1935: **North Gawber**, Barnsley, Yorkshire: (explosion)	19
21 March 1936: **Bardykes**, Glasgow, Lanarkshire: (roof fall)	5
26 May 1936: **Loveston**, Pembrokeshire: (inrush)	7
6 August 1936: **Wharncliffe Woodmoor**, Barnsley, Yorkshire: (explosion)	58
21 January 1937: **Markham**, Derbyshire: (explosion)	9
15 February 1937: **South Normanton**, Alfreton, Derbyshire : (explosions)	7
2 July 1937: **Holditch**, Newcastle, Staffordshire : (explosion)	30
30 January 1938: **Dumbreck**, Kilsyth, Stirlingshire: (fire)	9
20 April 1938: **Bank**, New Cumnock, Ayrshire: (haulage)	5
10 May 1938: **Markham (Blackshale Pit)**, Chesterfield, Derbyshire: (explosion)	79
6 June 1939: **Astley Green**, Tyldesley, Lancashire: (explosion)	6
28 October 1939: **Valleyfield**, Culross, Fife: (explosion)	35

Staffordshire mining communities continued to be badly affected by disasters. Fourteen miners were killed following an underground explosion at the Grove Colliery, Brownhills, on 1 October 1930, the event somewhat overshadowed with the 101 crash of the airship on the same day. This report extract, however, made part of a column in *The Times* newspaper two days later. A brief, c.20 seconds, newsreel extract showing the dramatic scenes on the pit top also survives and can be seen via www.itnsource.com.

Speaking at the official inquiry, the miners' leader A.J.Cook pressed unsuccessfully for the owners to be fined for infringing safety legislation in the 1911 Mines Act. Many of the victims were interred together in St James's church cemetery, and given 'military honours' as six of them were Great War heroes.

MIDLAND MINE EXPLOSION

FOURTEEN LIVES LOST

UNKNOWN CAUSE

(FROM OUR SPECIAL CORRESPONDENT)

BIRMINGHAM, Oct. 2

An explosion in which **14** men lost their lives took place at the Grove Colliery, in the South Staffordshire coalfield, about eight miles from Birmingham, last night. The news became public only this afternoon. The men were engaged in the removal of a coal-cutting machine at the coal face, about a mile and a half from the foot of the shaft, when for some reason as yet unknown the explosion took place. This morning the colliery owners, Messrs. Harrison, Limited, issued the following statement:—

The management very much regret to state that a serious explosion involving the loss of 14 lives occurred during the later part of the afternoon shift on October 1 in the shallow seam of their Grove Pit. The precise cause of the explosion is not yet known, but the matter is being carefully investigated by H.M. Inspector of Mines acting in conjunction with the management.

About **1,000** men are normally employed in the mine, but only the **14** who have lost their lives were in that part of

the pit where the explosion occurred. The time at which it happened can only

The fire and series of explosions at Holditch ('Brymbo') Colliery at Chesterton, in north Staffordshire, on the morning of 2 July 1937 was so serious that thirty brave men, the majority of whom involved in the post-incident safety and remedial work, lost their lives. One crucial issue that emerged was who had the ultimate responsibility for managing the colliery during the immediate crisis. According to law it was one man, the pit manager, who was John Owen Davies; but the joint managing director of the Holditch mine company, John Cocks, appears to have overruled Davies, the latter reluctantly acceding to his superiority regarding the best placing of the 'stoppings' to seal off the fire, locating them in an area where the most violent explosion then took place, killing all but eight of the thirty-five involved in the safety and recovery operation. This included Cocks himself, the pit's under manager H.L. Adkins, two mines inspectors, several volunteers and the 'stoppings men'. Three other miners had lost their lives a little earlier.

Another outstanding feature of the Holditch disaster concerned the immense courage of the pit rescue team, doing what they could in their breathing apparatus in terribly dangerous conditions over a 24-hour period. Many months later, on 27 March 1938, a crowd of two thousand, made up mostly of Holditch pitmen, witnessed a unique ceremony. The colliery rescue team were presented with a Sevres vase, medallion and diploma by Captain Crookshank MP, Secretary of the Mines Department, on behalf of the President of the French Republic. Years earlier, in 1906, at the Courreres mine in northern France, two-thirds of its workforce, 1,099 men and boys, died following an explosion and fires, Europe's worst mine disaster. The French were therefore well aware and most respectful of the importance of mine rescue work. The event received national press coverage.

Holditch Colliery.

On 5 August 1939 the *London Gazette* officially announced that Azarina (or 'Ezra') Clarke, overman and captain of the Holditch rescue team was awarded the prestigious Edward Medal in recognition of his gallantry when leading his team during the Holditch disaster. The commemoration included the following statement:

> 'The courage, initiative, endurance and qualities of leadership displayed by Clarke throughout the lengthy operations were outstanding.'

Ezra Clarke in later life.

This monument to the Holditch disaster, located outside Apedale Heritage Centre, incorporates a plaque commemorating the names of those who died. The centre is well worth a visit for anyone interested in Staffordshire mining, it contains many local items; and visitors can experience a realistic tour down the adjacent drift mine.

In memory of the thirty miners who lost their lives in the
Holditch Colliery Explosion
on July 2nd 1937

H.L. Adkins, 35	John Harvey, 39	Samuel Latham, 28
James Alfred Bloor, 51	John Hassell, 35	Abel Mayer, 39
John Cocks, 57	William Haystead, 45	Henry Mitchell, 44
Percy Condliffe, 35	William S. Hodkinson, 38	William Pepper, 39
Josiah Cooke, 37	W. Hough, 37	George T. Pickerill, 30
Albert Leslie Cooper, 30	Frederick John Howle, 36	Charles Price, 33
Albert Edward Cornes, 26	Reginald Jackson, 35	George T. Rushton, 41
Harold John Finney, 41	Harry Johnston, 34	Albert W. Seaton, 26
J.W. Forrester, 40	Ernest Jones, 51	Arthur R. Stanton, 31
T. Harris, 46	Thomas Henry Jones, 28	Frank Turner, 22

Mine disaster heroes

It is amazing how many individual miners and rescue teams came from from one coalfield area to another in order to help when a disaster struck. In 1935, on 22/23 August, ten lives were lost – including the supervisor of the Central Rescue Station – following a series of explosions in South Kirkby Colliery, a south Yorkshire pit. All six rescue workers had received burns when searching for a missing man, sadly found dead. But the situation would have been even more serious if not for the actions of more rescue men, including a 'Wiganer', James Pollitt, who was captain of one of the later-phase teams. Pollitt, along with Norman Baster and George Beamon were subsequently presented with Edward medals at Buckingham palace on 15 July 1936. Seventy years after the event, the daughter of James Pollitt, Margaret Banks, was presented with a replica bronze statue of a miner, which she gave to the town of Wigan. It is a small version of the 'South Kirkby miner' created by the Barnsley sculptor Graham Ibbeson in 2004-05 to commemorate all miners who died at the South Kirkby Colliery.

HONOURED: Margaret Banks (nee Pollitt) with the statue presented to the borough in memc ry of her father James's gallantry, pictured inset.

Mrs Maragert Banks.

'The South Kirkby miner' and its sculptor, Graham Ibbeson (left).

Gob fires

Spontaneous combustion of waste material (or 'gob'), placed on one side by working miners when getting the coal, continued to cause serious fires and explosions during the 1930s. At Manchester Collieries Limited's Astley Green Colliery, near Tyldsley in Lancashire, the outcome of attempts to extinguish a gob fire was the death of five experienced miners, including the pit's young manager, John Hewitt (aged 36), who had led the remedial operations. Several others were injured, one of them seriously. The event was headlined on the front page of the national newspaper *News Chronicle*, an illustration showing relatives and friends of the miners anxiously reading notices posted at the pit gates. An image of the late pit manager, taken 'just before he went underground' appeared on the front pages of several regional and local papers, this one from Newcastle's *The Journal*, published on 9 June, 1939. Details of Astley Green Colliery museum can be accessed via www.agcm.org.uk.

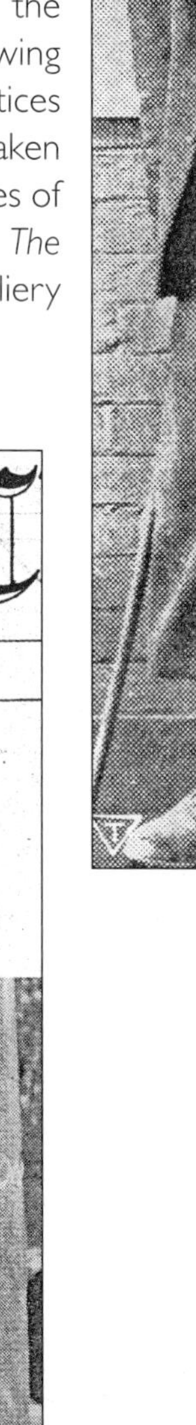

News C

No. 29,046 *** WEDNESDAY, JUNE 7, 1939

FIVE MEN DIE, FOUR INJURED, IN PIT FIRE EXPLOSIONS

Tommy Henwood and Black Friday at Bentley

The massive explosion caused by a gob fire deep in Bentley Colliery, near Doncaster, at 5.45 pm on Friday, 20 November 1931 accounted for the lives of forty-five miners, the majority dying in the pit, but some succumbing to terrible injuries and burns after being rescued. The tragedy continues to be commemorated every year, this image dating from 2003. The elderly man shown carrying a wreath is Tommy Henwood, who was guest of honour on the day. Tommy, who had started work at Bentley in 1924, was a pony-driver at the time of the disaster, and with his father helped to deploy sandbags and get out some of the bodies. Sadly, the search for five men had to be abandoned, the heat so intense that the affected area had to be sealed. Born in 1911, Tommy was the last known 'survivor', though not actually working on the fateful shift. Interviewed by the author after the 2003 commemoration, he passed away shortly afterwards.

On November 23rd 1931 a large crowd assembled at Arksey cemetery when over thirty of the deceased Bentley miners were interred in a mass grave. This postcard image was issued to mark the occasion.

After about a year, a large memorial stone was placed on the site of the graves, the occasion again commemorated by the publication of a postcard. After the 1978 paddy-mail disaster at Bentley Colliery an additional inscription was added to the memorial; and it is this memorial that is the focus of the annual service, which now commemorates both disasters.

Miners from Bentley Colliery, as well as the official rescue teams, operated with extraordinary bravery after the 1931 explosion. The bodies of most of the individuals brought out either dead or alive were in a terrible state due to burns and/or injuries. Afterwards the psychological impact on all concerned, included the many nurses and paramedics must have been long lasting if not permanent; indeed it was reported that some men never wished to work underground again. One of the last of the bodies recovered was that of Thomas Hopkinson, one of the pit's miners who was also a trained first-aider or 'ambulance man'. Thomas had apparently 'stayed behind' in order to attend to his wounded mates but was himself totally engulfed by the heat. Tom's widow received a posthumous Order of British Heroism award, presented by the 'workers' paper' the *Daily Herald*. The certificate included the phrase '...a brave man who in a moment of peril thought more of others than himself'. But in terms of gallantry recognition it was not the end of the story. For 'heroic acts of bravery', eight Edward medals were presented to Bentley rescuers and investigators – two of them meriting silver (First Class) awards – at a special investiture at Buckingham Palace on 16 February 1933.

Saddest of all: Gresford

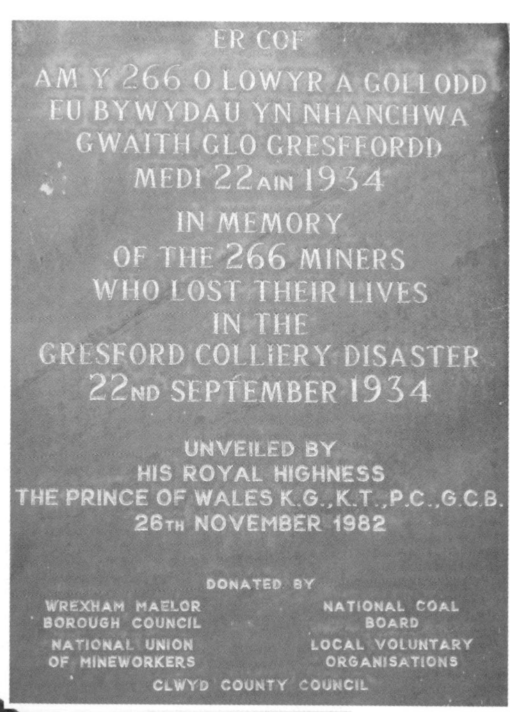

The tragedy that caused the greatest, most widespread and lasting sadness during the 1930s concerned the terrible disaster at Gresford, near Wrexham, which accounted for the deaths of 266 men and boys following an underground explosion and fire. Mounted within an unequalled-size pair of slate 'headstocks', a great pulley wheel forms the centrepiece of the Gresford disaster memorial, unveiled by the Prince of Wales near the site of the colliery in 1982. Below the commemorative plaque is a four-columned list of all the fatalities, in alphabetical order, some family names repeated many times: an extraordinary reminder of the real price of coal in Wales.

They say that a picture is worth a thousand words, perhaps so for this news image. A young woman wearing a fashionable hat, with her baby in a pram, looks away from the photographer in the direction of the pithead, her expression therefore unseen. Next to her a more mature man wearing a cap and raincoat, half-looking at her and the scene in front of him: men mostly, waiting for news close to the colliery head-frame, and a line of coal wagons emblazoned with a single word that was to be in the papers, on the radio and in newsreels: GRESFORD.

A few exhausted rescue workers walk away from Gresford pithead, the central figure glancing to his left towards a deputy, and perhaps one of the most hardworking and underrated people after disasters and accidents: a 'pit nurse'. Three of the Llay rescue team had been asphyxiated during the initial exploration, adding to the enormous toll of fatalities; and a pit top man lost his life when the cap of the sealed shaft blasted upwards due to great pressure of gas from below. Thus, the grim tally crept from 262 to 265 and finally 266. A last direct living link to Gresford – Eddie Edwards – a veteran who took part in the Gresford rescue operations, lived to the great age of 102, passing away on 6 January 2016.

After the explosion, just six miners escaped to safety; and only eleven miners' bodies were actually recovered. The underground conditions were so dreadful and dangerous that the mines inspectorate put an end to search and rescue, the eventual outcome being the entombment of most of those who had been working in the fateful Dennis area, about a mile from the pit bottom.

Numerous memorials and artworks to the Gresford disaster have appeared over the years. The inscribed plaque (1), sited above a metal cross on which a miner's lamp is entwined with a cord, can be seen in All Saints' Church. The artistic image (2) is a detail from an oil painting, an arched panel, created 'in memoriam' by Denise Bates in 1994.

Perhaps the most emotive and transferrable 'memorial' is 'The Miners' Hymn', known simply as *Gresford*, composed by Robert Saint (1905-1950 [image 3]) in 1936 and dedicated to the disaster victims. A former Hebburn, County Durham, miner, Saint was a talented musician who had received tuition from the the bandmaster of north Derbyshire's Creswell Colliery Band. Played at miners' galas and most evocatively at funeral and burial ceremonies of miners killed in accidents and disasters, an appreciation of Saint's life and work is part of Peter Crookston's *The Pitmen's Requiem* book (2010); and there is now an entry for Saint (by Robert Colls) in the *Oxford Dictionary of National Biography*. *Gresford* also features in Lee Hall's much-acclaimed play *The Pitmen Painters* and formed part of BBC Radio 4's Soul Music series of programmes (series 13, episode 2, 2012). Among the many versions available on YouTube, is one by the Grimethorpe Colliery Band recorded at Woodhorn Colliery Museum site, Ashington; and also a most appropriate Llay Welfare Band rendition, for BBC Wales.

1

2

3

Rescue workers wearing their Proto breathing apparatus, lamps and canaries prepare for another descent of North Gawber Colliery, near Barnsley on 12 September 1935, accompanied by a pit manager. Nineteen miners lost their lives – four dying in hospital – following an explosion that may have been caused by an ignition of gas during shot-firing.

Perhaps the most poignant image from the disaster was this one, reproduced on a postcard, showing the chalked message 'Farewell Fanny Old Pet xxx', discovered written on a piece of rock by the rescuers.

My father was a teenage miner at Wharncliffe Woodmoor (1,2 & 3) Colliery, located at the edge of the pit village of Carlton, near Barnsley, when an explosion resulted in fifty-eight fatalities on a black August morning in 1936. Another pit boy, Ron Palmer, was 'knocked-up' from his sleep in his parents' house three miles away, and told to rush to the colliery. Directed to go down the shaft by a deputy, Ron told me that his pit-bottom job was to write down the names of the stretchered bodies of his 'mates' as they were placed in the cage, a hurtful experience that he never got over. The first rare image shows the pit yard, soon to become a quagmire due to the pouring rain and many hundreds of tramping feet, taken by one of the crowd; and the pictures to the right are of Ron Palmer – about the time he did the pit bottom 'writing' – and in 2003 when interviewed by the author.

After the bodies from the Wharncliffe Woodmoor Colliery explosion were brought out of the pit they were placed on straw and taken to a temporary mortuary across the road from the pit, in the old Carlton Green school. There, they were washed by a small group of nurses. This image shows crowds and an ambulance waiting outside the old school.

Years later, Eleanor Bayley née Caswell recalled how she helped to 'clean' the bodies, prior to identification by relatives. It was a long, arduous and upsetting job. Nurse Caswell worked on the grim task alongside the local midwife and came across the latter's brother-in-law, who was only recognized after his face was washed; and Eleanor also discovered her Sunday-school teacher, as well as several former school friends. How distressing it must have been for her, aged just nineteen. Her father, Walter Caswell, a miner from the other pit in the village, was a first-aid instructor and helped with the rescue and recovery operations.

A young George Formby, already well-known but soon to become Britain's most famous singer-comedian and film star, visited Carlton following the Wharncliffe Woodmoor disaster. The main attraction at a fund raising concert at the Alhambra theatre, in Barnsley, Formby can be seen here (2nd right) wearing 'officials gear': helmet, waistcoat, shirt and tie; and carrying a deputy's stick and (partly visible in his left hand) miner's safety lamp, when visiting the colliery.

A large crowd containing many relatives and descendants of the fifty-eight miners who lost their lives in the Wharncliffe Woodmoor disaster, gathered near the site of the pit in 2008 in order to pay tribute to them; and also to witness the re-dedication of monuments and unveiling of a new information board. The project was the culmination of a wish to 'properly and respectfully remember' that sad August day in 1936 by Councillor Len Picken, the Mayor of Barnsley, himself a former local miner.

A runaway tub appears to have been the start of a chain of events that caused the explosion in the Blackshale seam of the Staveley company's Markham (No. 1) Colliery at 5.32 am on 10 May 1938, the vehicle cutting through a power cable; and the resultant sparks igniting disturbed dust. Of the 171 miners at work, 79 were killed and 40 seriously injured. Only fourteen months earlier, nine Markham miners lost their lives in an explosion in the same district of the mine. There are many stories concerning those who died in 1938, in the pit village of Duckmanton, where many of the miners lived badly affected, the event attracting widespread coverage in the local and national press. A short film showing the pit-top scene also appeared in cinemas, viewable online via British Pathe (www.britishpathe.com) or youtube. One extraordinary and perhaps forgotten aspect of the 'eve of war' disaster is that Adolf Hitler sent a telegram to the King expressing his sympathy with the relatives on behalf of the German people. Once again, George Formby appeared in concert to support the disaster fund.

Markham was such a big news story that an aircraft appears to have been commissioned to take photographs – such as this albeit grainy example – on the day of the disaster, several examples appearing in newspapers from Scotland to the south of England. Nevertheless, the gathering crowd as well as ambulances are discernible in the aerial shot. The smaller image shows desperate relatives – including schoolboys – scrutinizing the notice of fatalities posted at the pithead.

Across the Scottish coalfields fatal accidents continued on a regular basis during the 1930s, accounting for at least 1,250 deaths: over 125 every year on average. The most serious multiple-death example took place at the Fife Coal Company's Valleyfield pit on 28 October 1939, little more than a month after the start of the Second World War. At about four in the morning the sound and 'earthquake-like' tremors of a huge explosion caused great consternation in the neighbourhood of the pit. As a consequence of the 'Diamond' part of the mine 'firing', 33 miners were killed outright and two others were fatally injured. Only a month earlier, John Sloan, the pit's under-manager, lost his life in a roof fall, when inspecting the same district of the mine. Despite the wartime reportage, the disaster was given some coverage in regional and national newspapers. This pithead image, showing the gathering crowd – including what appears to be a man in military uniform – is from the *Aberdeen Journal* of 30 October.

Among the stories about the Valleyfield colliery disaster, the most tragic relates to Thomas Kerr (aged 58). Conveyed to hospital after crawling his way away out of the danger area, Kerr was apparently told that his son (Thomas Kerr jnr, 27) had perished in the disaster; but Kerr himself died shortly afterwards. Another, more heartening tale concerned a pumpman, David Anderson. Almost unconscious due to the presence of post-explosion gas, Anderson shouted to ten other men to crawl the 500 yards toward 'his pump' in the Culress section of the mine. There, the rotating blades provided rushes of air so that the men could breathe. A hero by most interpretations, Anderson probably said that he did what miners always do in times of crisis: come to help others in dire need.

Exhausted rescue men stretcher the body of a miner after searching underground at Valleyfield Colliery.

A commemorative service was held to honour those who perished at the Valleyfield colliery in 2014, on the 75th anniversary of the disaster. Those paying their respects included Councillor Kate Stewart who laid a wreath in memory of her granddad, Jarvis McFadzean, who was 28 when he was killed.

Chapter Five

1940-1949
War to Nationalisation

The decade from 1940 to 1949 witnessed far less mine disasters than previously, in fact it was the lowest decennial number (20) since the start of the century; and although the total of 'disaster-deaths' were a little higher than in the 1920s, the situation would have been – statistically – far better but for a huge incident at Whitehaven's William Pit in Cumberland.

And yet, accidents as a whole continued to take place at very unacceptable levels, despite increased efforts to make coalmining a much safer industry. During the war years (1939-45), 5,394 men and boys were killed in all types of mining accidents, and almost 20,000 seriously injured. If accidents where miners were off work for at least three days are included, the total figure rises to an astonishing 1,062,122. Add deaths from respiratory causes during the same period, around 4,000 known cases, then 'mining' continued to be an unhealthy and dangerous occupation.

Coal as a source of energy was in great demand again due to both military and domestic needs but it took urgent legislation to stop a great drift of men away from the mines, which was not too surprising given the conditions of work and the facts given in the previous paragraph. By the spring of 1941, manpower had fallen to less than 700,000 for the first time in the modern era and to combat the 'coal crisis' miners were not allowed to leave their employment without permission of the National Service office; and in 1943 so-called 'Bevin Boys' – thousands of young men aged 18-25 – were conscripted by ballot into the pits.

The push to mine coal for the war effort may well have increased the risk of accidents, miners working what hours that they could in conditions where a relatively small mishap could become a major tragedy within seconds and minutes. The worst instance occurred at Sneyd Colliery in north Staffordshire on New Year's Day, 1942.

On a positive note, the establishment of the Mines Medical Service in 1944 and the formation of the National Union of Mineworkers in the same year, were welcomed by most people who wanted a better organised and safer industry. The nationalisation process, begun in earnest in 1946, came to fruition on 1 January 1947 when flags proclaiming 'people ownership' were hoisted above pit pulley wheels. The enthusiasm for change was welcomed by most of the miners, though the dream was subsequently shattered when the new National Coal Board began to close so many of their collieries; accidents and disasters by were no means reduced to 'acceptable' levels.

Another 'improvement', a long time coming, was the establishment of the Miners' Special Fatal Accident Fund in 1948, to help alleviate the loss of family income following an accident and to provide financial help to dependants.

The research facilities near Buxton and Sheffield continued their technical and scientific experiments in respect of mine safety, the latter in particular, with its association with the mine department at Sheffield University, becoming of world importance, from 1946 known as the Safety in Mines Research Establishment (SMRE), within the Ministry of Power. The establishment of national first aid competitions now ran alongside the many regional and local schemes, providing further stimulation – if ever it was needed – for 'interested' miners themselves to receive medical training for use in emergencies.

The Yorkshire coalfield was badly affected by disasters, with eight (40%) of all 5-plus fatality accidents during the 1940s, the most serious at Crigglestone Colliery when twenty-two miners died. But it was the smaller coalfields that fared the worst, especially around Whitehaven in Cumberland, where three tragic events once again demonstrated how vulnerable miners were when working the thin and dangerously gassy seams there. The William Pit disaster of 1947, already referred to above, was a massive single event, at a mine referred to by authors Ray Devlin and Harry Fancy as 'the most dangerous pit in the kingdom', in their historic account (Friends of Whitehaven Museum, 2003 and 2015) of the colliery, the disaster also described in detail in Amanda Garraway's '104 Men' publication (2007). The old coalfield in Durham, 'quiet' in disaster terms during the previous decade, experienced a trio of multiple-death tragedies, at Sacriston, Murton and Louisa collieries, accounting for forty lives.

The 'heroic endeavours' of miners and rescue workers continued to be recognised by a variety of official and voluntary bodies; tributes to individual miners and rescue teams were an almost common feature of the newspaper reports. More than twenty Edward medals were awarded, four of them for the great bravery evident at the Louisa Colliery disaster, three of these felt to be so outstanding that they were of silver (First Class) status.

Edward Medal.

Timeline of coal mine disaster fatalities (5+), 1940-49

Event	Fatalities
21 March 1940: **Mossfield**, Longton, Staffordshire: (explosion)	11
5 June 1940: **Upton**, Pontefract, Yorkshire: (explosion)	9
4 December 1940: **Sacriston**, County Durham: (stone fall)	5
3 June 1941: **William Pit**, Whitehaven, Cumberland: (explosion)	12
24 June 1941: **Kiveton Park**, Rotherham, Yorkshire: (explosion)	5
10 July 1941: **Rhigos**, Gyn Neath, Glamorganshire: (explosion)	16
29 July 1941: **Crigglestone**, Wakefield, Yorkshire: (explosion)	22
19 October 1941: **Bullcroft**, Doncaster, Yorkshire: (explosion)	6
25 November 1941: **Blaenclydach**, Glamorganshire: (explosion)	7
1 January 1942: **Sneyd**, Staffordshire: (explosion)	57
5 January 1942: **Plank Lane**, Bickershaw, Lancashire: (explosion)	6
16/17 February 1942: **Barnsley Main**, Yorkshire: (explosion)	13
26 June 1942: **Murton**, County Durham: (explosion)	13
4 March 1945: **Manvers Main**, Rotherham, Yorkshire: (explosion)	5
9 December 1946: **Lowca (Harrington)**, Cumberland: (explosion)	15
10 January 1947*: **Burngrange**, West Calder, Midlothian: (explosion)	15
7 May 1947: **Barnsley Main**, Yorkshire: (explosion)	9
15 August 1947: **William Pit**, Whitehaven, Cumberland: (explosion)	104
22 August 1947: **Louisa**, Stanley, County Durham: (explosion)	22
9 September 1947: **Ingham,** Dewsbury, Yorkshire: (explosion)	12

**shale mine*

On the night of 16 February 1942, an explosion and fire occurred in the Fenton seam, at Barnsley Main, two men working in the area received serious burns, and one, Fred Wood, so badly affected that he died in hospital. A 'flash' from a trailing coal-cutter cable ignited gas, according to the official inquiry. Unfortunately, during remedial work to make the workings safe, a second, greater explosion occurred. Of the sixty-two men underground making and overseeing the erection of 'stoppings' to seal off the dangerous areas of the mine, twelve lost their lives, among them the pit's under-manager John Albert Harrott who had worked there from the age of 14.

The late 'Reg' Batterham worked with the two men initially affected by the first explosion but managed to escape without serious injury. When in his eighties, speaking to the author in 2009, Reg recalled his experiences and the lamentable circumstances of the disaster – as though it had taken place yesterday. The other very rare unofficial image is of a miner at work 'cleaning out the gummings [waste]' in Barnsley Main, shovelling in front of a coal-cutter; and notice the attached cable.

It is remarkable that many true stories concerning pit disasters remain in family memories and are not available in any published accounts. When he was just three years old, Aidan Bell was so impressed by the bravery of his grandfather, William Bell, that Willliam remained an heroic figure in his eyes, and inspired him to a 46-year-long career in mining. William Bell was concussed at the return stopping in Barnsley Main after the disaster of 1942. In a 'dead-like' state, he would almost certainly have been left by the initial sweep taken by the rescue team but for one circumstance: his leg twitched, indicating that he was still alive, his pit trousers having been set alight earlier. After three days in Barnsley's 'miners' hospital' (Beckett's), William was sent home and was able to show a very impressionable grandson his burn-affected right leg. A vital personal requisite, William's false teeth, were found in the main return. William had migrated to Barnsley from Durham in 1924 and, a certified under-manager, aged 65, was still working as a safety officer at Barnsley Main. Interestingly, and as a further mark of his bravery in Aidan's eyes, he had been involved in the 'body-recovery' of the search and rescue operations at the Burns Pit, West Stanley during the terrible disaster there in 1909.

Born into a mining family at Waterhouses in County Durham, this cabinet-style studio photograph is of William Bell when he was a young man.

The second disaster at Barnsley Main occurred only a few months after nationalisation, at 12.15 pm on Wednesday 7 May 1947, when an explosion in the new Kent seam resulted in the deaths of nine experienced miners aged 25-54. Once again, a trailing cable appears to have been the source of the ignition, though no case of criminal neglect was given at the inquest or inquiry, despite the comments of the miners' leader, Joe Hall. The colliery actually resumed work the day after the explosion, coal production deemed so vital for the country.

Two rescue men, Sydney Blackburn (shot-firer) and Harry Crummack (chargeman filler) were awarded Edward medals (bronze) for leading a group of men to safety and then returning to save the lives of two of their mates. Exhausted, they nevertheless only agreed to return to the surface after rescue teams arrived.

Several of the families affected by the two Barnsley disasters lived in the parish of Ardsley, where William Bell was one of the churchwardens. A memorial plaque to the twelve men who were killed on 17 July; and also of nine others who lost their lives in the 1947 disaster can be seen inside the parish church (Christ Church).

The explosion that ripped through the No.1 West District of Crigglestone Colliery towards the end of the afternoon shift on Tuesday 29 July 1941 was so violent and gaseous that twenty-two of the twenty-five miners lost their lives, and the remaining three were injured. Among the deceased were three brothers of the Fox family. Compensation for widows and dependants of disasters continued to be *ad hoc* and meagre. The sum of £5 was sent to the widows by the pit's owners, the Benzol and By-Products Company Limited, and the miners themselves (about 800) agreed to contribute two shillings (20p) each for eleven weeks to assist the widows and dependants. With many of the deceased young married men with children, it must have been very hard indeed for families to survive during the already poverty-affected war years. Robert White, for instance, left five children.

(1)

22 LIVES LOST IN PIT EXPLOSION

FROM OUR CORRESPONDENT

WAKEFIELD, JULY 30

It is now known that 22 men were killed and three injured at Crigglestone Colliery, near Wakefield, as a result of the explosion [reported in the later editions of *The Times*] on Tuesday night in the south district Haigh Moor seam.

The colliery, which is operated by Benzol Products, Limited, employs 800 men. Late this afternoon all but six bodies had been brought to the surface.

The identity of those killed was partly established by disks on the men's clothing, but a general identification was held to-day at the village hall, which has been turned into a mortuary.

Explosion in Yorkshire Pit

20 Men Trapped

From Our Own Correspondent

WAKEFIELD, Wednesday

THE fate of over 20 miners two miles from the pit bottom at Crigglestone Colliery, near Wakefield, hung in the balance at dawn this morning.

About 8 o'clock last night there was an explosion in the southern district where some 30 miners were working. Immediately work at the colliery was suspended to permit rescue workers going to the scene of the explosion.

Three Brothers Among Victims

Twenty-two miners lost their lives in an explosion which occurred on Tuesday night at Grigglestone Colliery, near Wakefield, Yorkshire.

All but six of the bodies have been brought to the surface. Among the dead are three brothers, James Arthur Fox, of Thornhill Lees, Dewsbury, and Lloyd and Bernard Fox, of Middlestown, near Wakefield.

Another victim, Robert White, is an old Wakefield Trinity Rugby League footballer.

Three men were injured. One of them, named Broadhead, told his wife in hospital yesterday that he was blown 40 yards.

A rescue worker said that coal tubs had been thrown about like match boxes.

Despite the war, the disaster was reported, albeit briefly, in many of the national and regional newspapers. These extracts are from (1) *The Times;* (2) *Yorkshire Post* and (3) *Western Daily Express* (Scotland) on 30-31 July 1941.

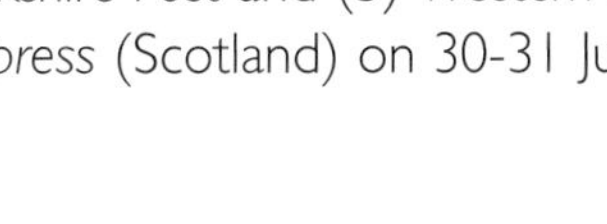

Staffordshire was hit by two serious underground explosions during the war years, the first at Mossfield, Longton, on 21 March 1940 when eleven miners died, including a father and son: Roland Porter (55) and Richard Porter (27). Among the victims was a 16-year-old haulage hand, Leslie Leake. Later, the colliery owners' representative gave out twenty £1 notes to each of the widows and mothers 'to help relieve the distress'.

The second disaster, at Sneyd (No.4 pit), near Burslem, on New Year's Day 1942, in its scale and family stories was even more tragic. Here, as elsewhere, the miners were doing what they could to mine coal for the 'war effort', even working on a 'holiday day'. The fifty-seven men and youths who lost their lives made this the worst mine disaster in Britain during the second World War years. The youngest of the deceased, David Briggs, was only 15 years old and two teenage brothers, Frank (18) and Alex Harrison (17) died. Once again, a father and son were among the fatalities: James Bennett (41) and George Bennett (19). A 65-year-old miner, Hamlett Briggs was the oldest to die. Occurring at about 7.50 am in the Seven Feet Banbury seam, most of the miners that were killed were young family men, with an average age of just 31 years. Due to the great efforts of the local search and rescue teams, all the bodies were recovered by 9 January.

Sneyd, despite being the scene of a great disaster, was one of the most modern collieries in the North Staffordshire coalfield. It ceased production in 1962.

51 MISSING IN COLLIERY

MEN TRAPPED AFTER EXPLOSION

SEVEN BODIES RECOVERED

FROM OUR CORRESPONDENT

HANLEY, STAFFS, JAN. 1

Seven men are dead and 51 missing as the result of an explosion at the Sneyd Collieries, Burslem, Stoke-on-Trent, to-day. It was stated to-night that there was no hope for the missing men.

The trapped men were working in the 7ft. Banbury seam of No. 4 pit. Rescue work began immediately after the explosion, which

EXPLOSION IN COAL MINE

58 MEN FEARED DEAD

Fifty-eight men are feared to have lost their lives in an explosion which occurred at Sneyd Collieries, Burslem, Stoke-on-Trent, yesterday. The bodies of seven men were quickly recovered, but 51 others were entombed and late last night it was stated that there was no hope for them. When rescue work was suspended until the morning five more bodies had been found. The cause of the explosion is unknown, but there was no outbreak of fire.

Our Hanley Correspondent's account of the disaster appears on page 2.

The initial news of the Sneyd disaster, reported the day after in daily newspapers, was that seven men were dead and more than fifty 'missing' or trapped; but the full extent of the disaster soon emerged. The headlines shown below relate to an account in *The Times* of 2 January 1942.

A set of runaway tubs appears to have started a chain of tragic events in Sneyd Colliery, the final outcome being a massive 'coal dust-related' explosion from a shower of sparks.

A 'special report' in the *Daily Mirror*, made much of the great sacrifice that the miners had made 'winning coal for you, for ships, for munition and other war factories', referring to the disaster victims (58 rather than the actual 57) as 'FRONT-LINE WORKERS', the account illustrated by a small image showing children waiting for news at the gate of the colliery. With hindsight, patriotism may have verged with journalistic propaganda at the time, but the fact remains that the Sneyd miners really were working on News Year's Day in response to a great national demand for increase production, and this should never be forgotten.

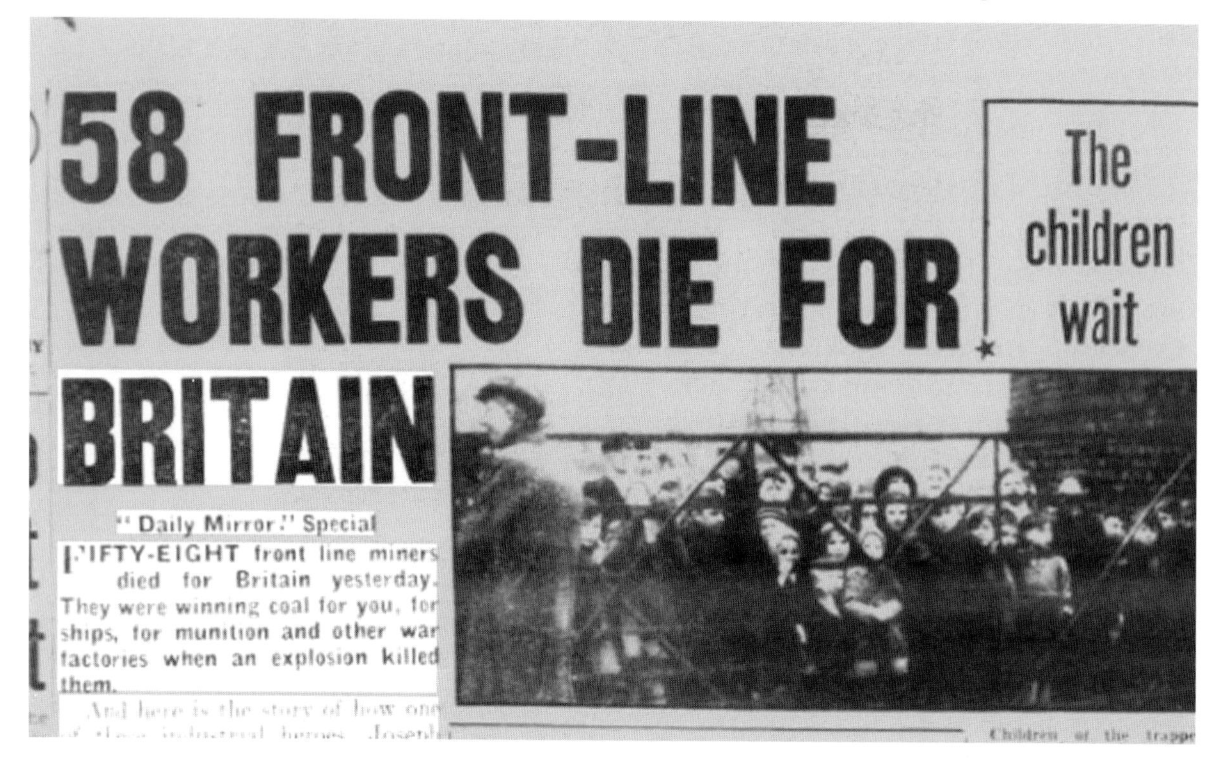

58 FRONT-LINE WORKERS DIE FOR BRITAIN

"Daily Mirror" Special

FIFTY-EIGHT front line miners died for Britain yesterday. They were winning coal for you, for ships, for munition and other war factories when an explosion killed them.

The children wait

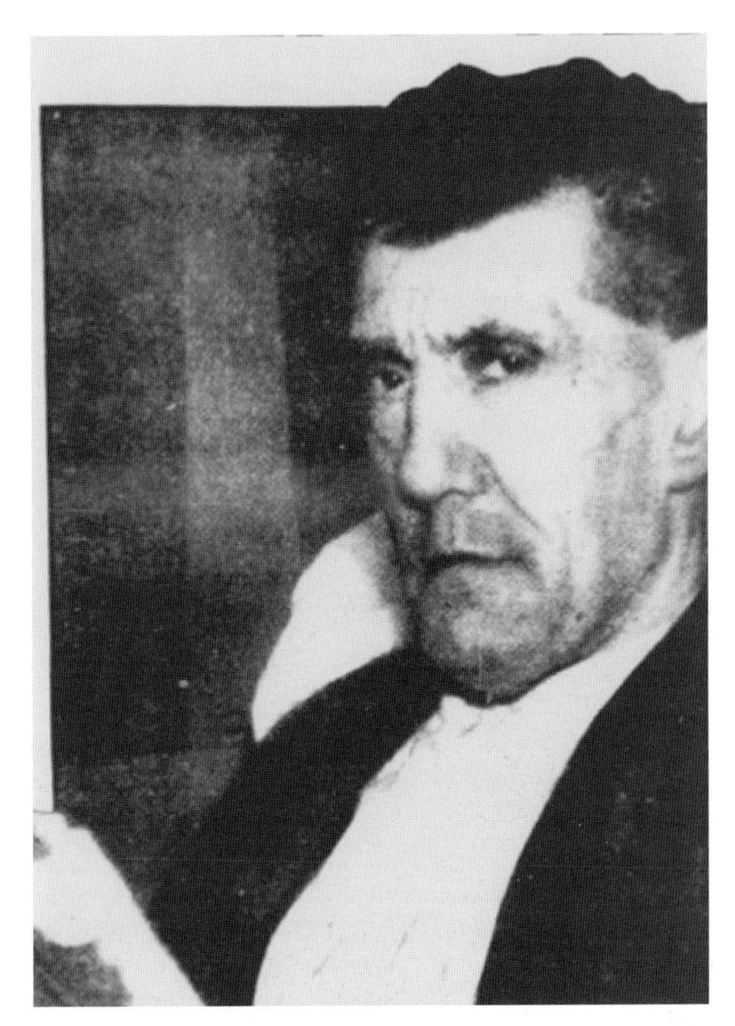

Several stories relating to individual victims and survivors of the Sneyd disaster appeared in the press. One prominent account concerned the 'great escape' of 64-year-old Tom Gibson, who was able to use his vast local experience of the mine by crawling about two-hundred yards along a narrow passageway into the Holly Lane district of the pit. The *Daily Mirror,* in particular, made much of the 'lucky one' under the headline 'HE WAS LEFT ALIVE', believed to be the only survivor; and saying that he had been 'hewing the vital war product out of the earth' at the time of the explosion. An interesting story concerned a young haulage hand, 'Jack' Bailey, who had been presumed dead but walked into the Miners' Hall (or 'pit offices', depending on the report) to tell and show officials that he was very much alive and well. Bailey had only arrived to work at the pit from Yorkshire a few days before the disaster, moving to the area to assist hospitalized 'in-laws'. The latter got a shock when their 'dead' son-in-law walked into the ward to collect them. Apparently the blast from the explosion had knocked off his hard hat and badge but he was unhurt and able to get out of the mine. There were two other survivors.

HEROES of SNEYD

City Voices Writers' Group

HEROES of SNEYD is a filmed record of the moving performance given by the City Voices Writers' Group of an original script by their co-founder Paul Williamson and produced by Alan Barnett – performed in Holy Trinity Church, Sneyd, near to the former site of Sneyd Colliery. The group is a mix of poets, short story writers and script/play writers, and they have raised thousands of pounds for local and national charities over the last ten years.

The documentary following is dedicated to the memory of the 57 men and boys who lost their lives on New Year's Day, 1942. The explosion at Sneyd is put into the context of wartime, explained by experts at Apedale Heritage Centre and discussed by local historians. There are interviews with many local people involved in the disaster, family and friends of the men lost – and tributes to the rescue team.

The DVD ends with Keith Meeson's final fund-raising walk to all the six town halls of the Potteries, and the achievement and unveiling of the Memorial to the Disaster in Market Square, Burslem, in 2007 - with key speeches and a range of interviews.

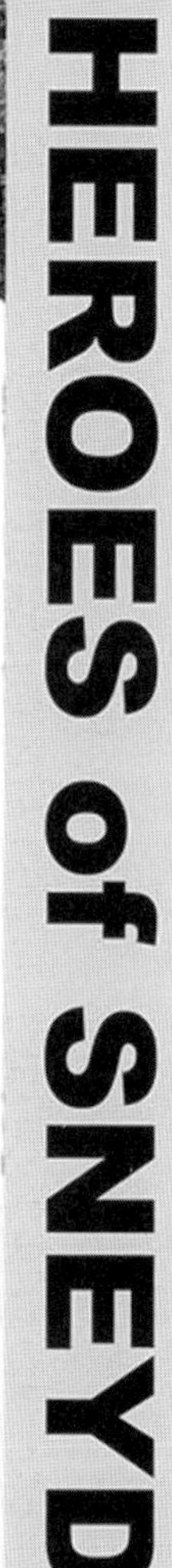

120min

A new memorial to the miners who lost their lives at Sneyd (and to the work of the rescue teams) was erected across from Burslem Town Hall in 2007. This excellent tribute DVD includes a documentary containing oral testimony.

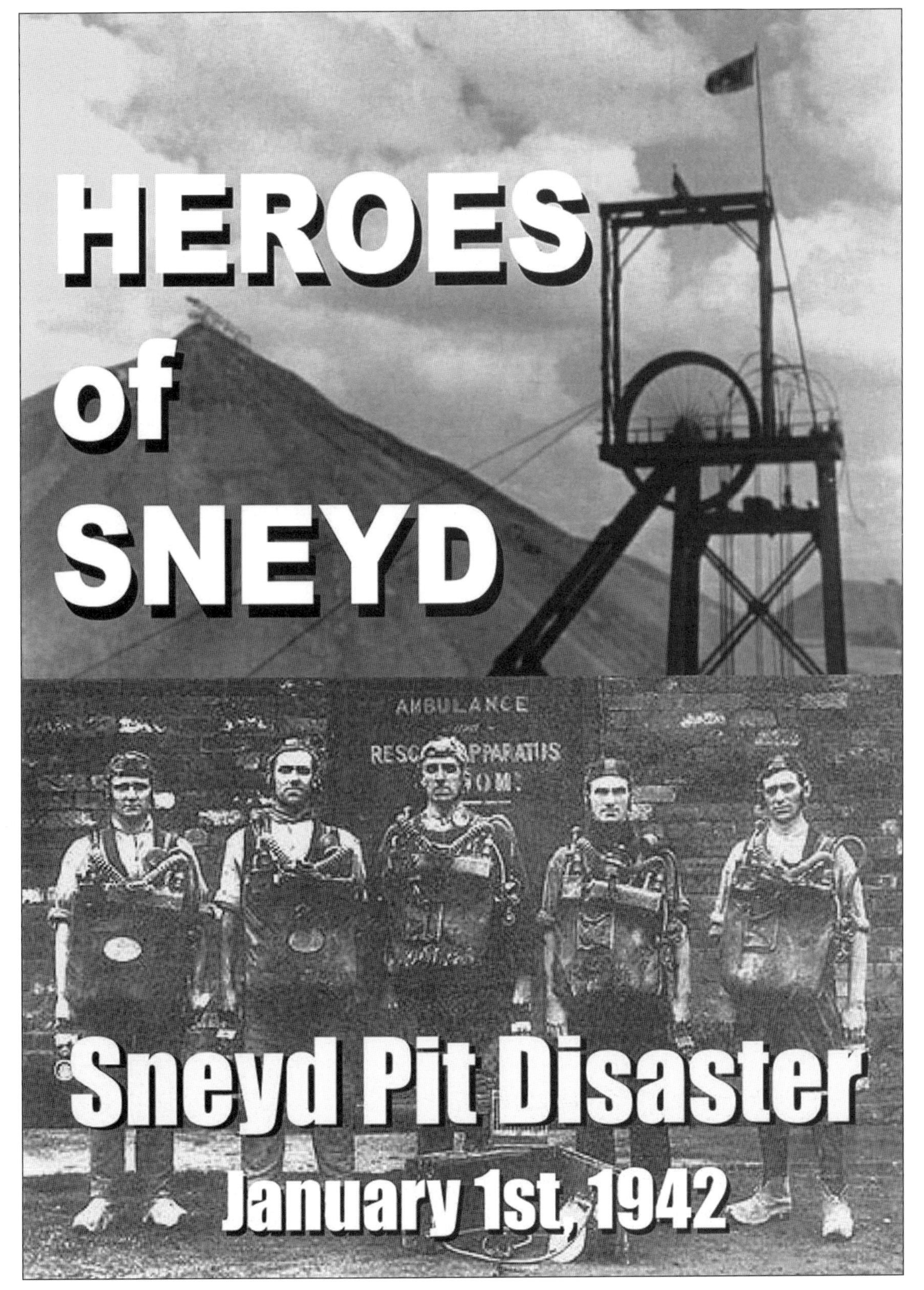

By kind permission of Ray Johnson MBE: Director, Staffordshire Film Archive (www.filmarchive.org.uk)

Less than a week after Sneyd, just before midnight on 5 January 1942, six men lost their lives in the 'Rise Unit' of No.4 pit of Bickershaw Collieries' Plank Lane mine, near Leigh, Lancashire. An explosion had occurred in an already sealed-off (therefore potentially dangerous) area. The colliery had a recent history of serious accidents. Nine years earlier, in 1932, in No. 3 pit, a cage crashed to the pit bottom due to an 'overwind', nineteen of the men drowning in the sump; and two years later five men and a boy miner were killed through an explosion caused by shot-firing. Among the six dead in 1942 were the night manager, Thomas Monaghan (40) and safety officer, John Dykes (38). The inquest jury returned a verdict of 'death from misadventure' for all six of the victims but also accepted the views of the mine manager, James French, that spontaneous combustion in the sealed area was the likely cause of an explosion of firedamp (gas).

SIX DEAD IN LEIGH PIT

SURVIVOR'S STORY OF STRUGGLE TO SAFETY

THREE MEN TAKEN TO HOSPITAL

Six men were killed and four injured, three detained in hospital, as the result of an explosion at the No. 4 pit, Plank Lane Colliery, Leigh, shortly before midnight on Monday.

The cause of the explosion is thought to have been a "blow-out" of gas near where the men were working.

A survivor told how suspicions that all was not well arose amongst a party of men, and of his subsequent struggle to a place where the air was fresher.

This was the headline in the *Leigh Journal* of 9 January 1942. The image of John Dykes is taken from the resumed inquest report, dated 16 January 1942, in the same newspaper.

On 3 June 1941 people living within a 'hearing distance' of William Pit at Whitehaven were left in doubt that there had been a serious accident, the repeated blasts from the steam horn preceding a great rush of people to the mine. An explosion had occurred at 2.15 pm, almost three miles from the pit bottom, when a 'stopping team' were endeavouring to seal off a dangerous part of the mine. During this process water was being pumped and sprayed in order to cool a 'heatings area' but this was the start of a cataclysmic event, 'water gas' (vaporization) combining with spontaneous combustion, an extremely rare if not unique situation. The outcome was the deaths of twelve miners, whilst eleven others received serious injuries.

Among the fatalities was 19-year-old Robert ('our Bob') McGrievy, a haulage lad who lived with his parents. The McGrievy family had an association with William Pit going back several generations, including women and girls who worked on the pit-top screens. Robert's father, John McGrievy, born in 1893, and shown here, was the subject of one of W.H. Freeth's series of 'pit profiles' (No.29), published in the September 1949 issue of the NCB's *Coal News* magazine. John's mining career at William started when working underground at a lamp relighting station at the age of fourteen, progressing to becoming an overman; and his interest in ambulance and rescue work was such that he became the pit's safety training officer and first aid instructor. Freeth shows McGrievy in his pit clothes, leaning slightly on a wall, his safety lamp hanging from his trouser belt. Such expertise and leadership were in great demand on a grim August day only two years earlier when William Pit experienced its worst ever disaster.

Blasts from a pit horn meant only one outcome for Whitehaven on an otherwise lovely summer evening on 15 August 1947: a great and fearful rush of people to the pithead. It was the third and by far the most serious 'explosion-disaster' at 'William' in the twentieth century; and nationwide the last (of eight) 100-plus-fatality disasters. The tragedy was covered in detail by the press and media of the day, with moving images reaching cinema audiences through British Pathe (viewable online today). The headlines shown below were typical of those that appeared in the 'dailies' on the day after the disaster, Saturday 16 August, 1947, taken from the same or similar local sources; and at a time when the full circumstances were not known. Whilst there was much common reportage, editors and journalists also provided their own interpretation and commentary. This small sample is from *The Times* (1), *Dundee Courier* (2), *Sunderland Daily Echo* (3) and *Gloucester Echo* (4).

111 MINERS TRAPPED AFTER EXPLOSION

RESCUE DELAYED BY ROOF FALLS

Rescue workers early to-day were digging their way towards 111 miners trapped by an explosion yesterday in William pit, Whitehaven, which runs under the sea off the Cumberland coast.

One hundred and twenty-one men were in the pit when the explosion caused heavy falls of roof at about 5.40 p.m. Ten are known to be safe.

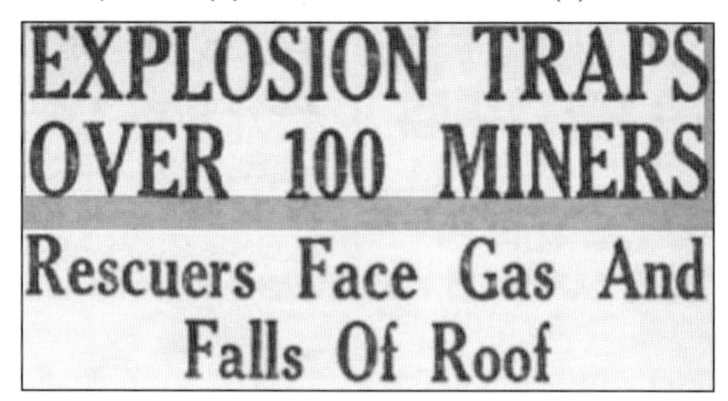

EXPLOSION TRAPS OVER 100 MINERS

Rescuers Face Gas And Falls Of Roof

2

DISASTER PIT

111 Death Roll is Feared

AFTER AN ALL-NIGHT VIGIL, WEEPING WOMEN AND SILENT MEN CONTINUE TO CROWD THE YARD OF THE WILLIAM PIT AT WHITEHAVEN TO-DAY AS THEY WAIT FOR NEWS OF HUSBANDS, SONS, AND SWEETHEARTS AMONG THE MINERS STILL ENTOMBED BY YESTERDAY'S SHATTERING UNDERSEA EXPLOSION. LITTLE HOPE IS NOW HELD OUT FOR THEM

FUEL MINISTER

3

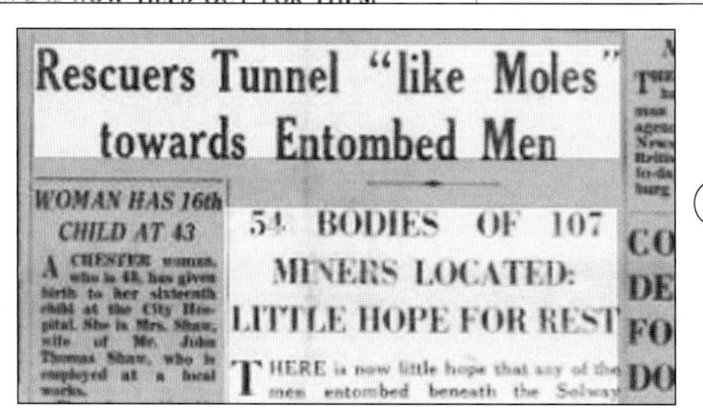

Rescuers Tunnel "like Moles" towards Entombed Men

WOMAN HAS 16th CHILD AT 43

A CHESTER woman, who is 43, has given birth to her sixteenth child at the City Hospital. She is Mrs. Shaw, wife of Mr. John Thomas Shaw, who is employed at a local works.

54 BODIES OF 107 MINERS LOCATED: LITTLE HOPE FOR REST

THERE is now little hope that any of the men entombed beneath the Solway

'Whitehaven in the news, continued...'

Some regional newspapers managed to include photographs as part of their coverage the day after the disaster. A 'grainy' example (1) appeared on the front page of the Leeds-based *Yorkshire Evening Post* (YEP), the descriptive including: '...relatives of men entombed in the Whitehaven mine wait in the shadow of the shaft head for news from the rescue party...'. The YEP's main headline and report, however, focused on the three 'trapped miners' who managed to 'walk out' of 'Whitehaven Death Pit' (2), a story that was also covered in many of the local/regional papers, and some nationals. The three escapees (3) had been working in the No. 2 Rise District when the explosion occurred. The most experienced of the three, Birkett, was able to lead them away from danger via a higher roadway, the men wearing impromptu gas masks from scarves or stockings.

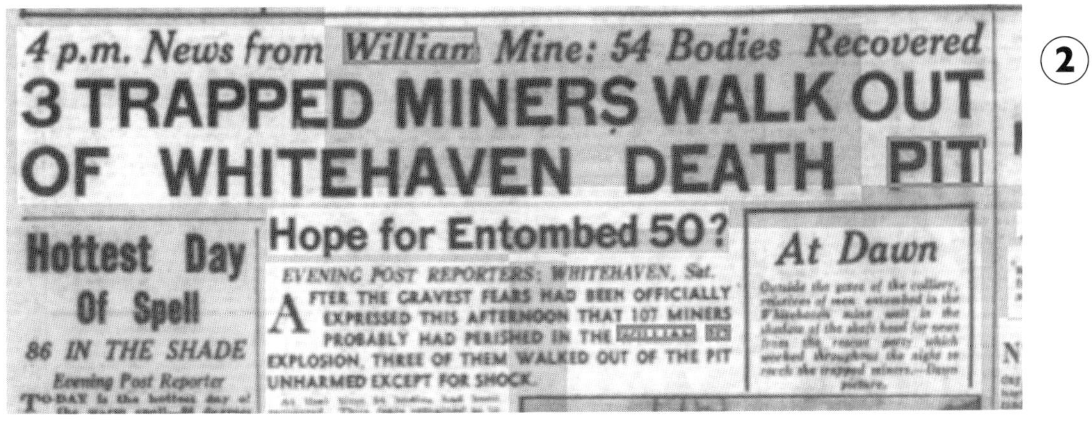

4 p.m. News from William Mine: 54 Bodies Recovered

3 TRAPPED MINERS WALK OUT OF WHITEHAVEN DEATH PIT

Hottest Day Of Spell

86 IN THE SHADE

Evening Post Reporter

Hope for Entombed 50?

EVENING POST REPORTERS: WHITEHAVEN, Sat.

AFTER THE GRAVEST FEARS HAD BEEN OFFICIALLY EXPRESSED THIS AFTERNOON THAT 107 MINERS PROBABLY HAD PERISHED IN THE [illegible] [illegible] EXPLOSION, THREE OF THEM WALKED OUT OF THE PIT UNHARMED EXCEPT FOR SHOCK.

At Dawn

(2)

(1)

(3)

Whitehaven 'in the news' continued...

Rescue teams from Durham and Northumberland arrived at 'William' to assist and work in shifts with the Cumberland crews in what soon became 'search for bodies' operations. Over a hundred underground explorations took place often in very difficult and dangerous conditions. It is important for us to remember that these men were volunteers who gave up their time to train in mines rescue and first aid. This image shows a team, believed to be from Ashington, examining a caged canary, a vital piece of 'kit' for the searches for gas detection, along with their breathing apparatus and safety lamps.

An unusual aspect of the 1947 William Pit disaster was the use of dogs during the search and rescue operations. The *Daily Mail* reported that three Alsations (German Shepherds) 'specially trained in finding people buried under air-raid debris' arrived at the pit at 2 am on 18 August. They were named as Jet, Rex and Prince. Five-year-old Jet had won the new Dickin Medal ('the animal's VC) after finding and saving the lives of air-raid victims in the London blitz. The image displayed above, placed in the *Yorkshire Post and Leeds Intelligencer* on 20 August 1947, shows George Cameron of Clifton (No.1) rescue team with two of the dogs, Jet by George. The dogs accompanied teams searching for the last few bodies left in the mine.

The Dickin Medal (also shown below), instituted in 1943, was named after the founder of the People's Dispensary for Sick Animals, Maria Dickin. A recent (2016) awardee is 'Lucca', also an Alsation, who lost a leg in a roadside bomb blast while serving with the US military in Afghanistan.

Expert opinion as to the cause of the explosion focused on a deputy firing a shot in the roof of a 'waste' area, gas being then ignited in a 'break' in the shot hole (No.3) on the right of No.2 Dip Longwall Face, the subsequent flames spreading through 2,000 yards of roadways.

Although 'no blame to any one person or system' was given, the West Cumberland coroner in his concluding remarks stressed the great importance of 'every man doing his job thoroughly and well', as this affected the lives of everyone at work in the mine. The management needed to use more adequate guidelines and supervision of such work in future; and the ventilation of the mine also needed attention as there had been breaches of mine safety regulation. In 1949, the new National Coal Board, in an out of court settlement to many of the dependants, did not accept any liability for the accident.

Two late widows: Murial Pollitt (previously Williamson) and Mary Broach (previously Murray) display a commemorative list of the disaster victims at St John's Church in 1997. Murial had been married for 22 months to William Williamson when he lost his life in the pit, aged 27. It was the first birthday of their son David and they were looking forward to a holiday. William had previously served in the forces. Mary had been married eleven years when her 39-year old husband 'Billy' was killed. She had asked him not to go to work, a premonition that proved to be correct. Courtesy of the Whitehaven News (50th anniversary of William Pit disaster supplement, 1997).

The old Durham coalfield had escaped explosion-type disasters for almost forty years until the 1940s when a shot-firing accident in Murton Colliery on Friday 26 June 1942 resulted in the deaths of thirteen men. And then, also on a Friday, at the Louisa (Morrison) Pit on 22 August 1947, barely eight months after the nationalisation of the mines and only a week after the 'William' disaster, twenty-two night-shift men lost their lives following a small explosion of firedamp, which was enhanced by the presence of coal dust. Conclusive evidence showed that 'smoking' was the cause of the ignition, almost certainly from a match having been struck to light a cigarette; in fact, similar 'contraband' was found in the pockets of several of the deceased miners. The youngest fatality was Walter Roe (18) and the oldest, John Rowland (55).

Louisa Pit, near Stanley, looking neat and well-ordered in this postcard image, was one of many collieries closed by the NCB in the 1960s.

A remarkable feature of the Louisa Pit tragedy was the courage of three deputies (Harry Robinson, Joseph Shanley and William Younger), who were working on safety operations in another seam at the time of the explosion. Ignoring their own personal safety, they proceeded to the source of the explosion, where they were joined by an experienced overman, John Hutchinson. Their repeated efforts resulted in ten of the incapacitated men to be brought out, five of them still alive (though two died later). Conditions were so bad that the beams of the rescuers cap lamps barely shone a foot or so through the darkness. All four men were subsequently awarded certificates of merit from the Carnegie Hero Fund and each also received prestigious Edward medals (First Class), presented to them at Buckingham Palace the following summer (and 'converted' to the George Cross in 1971).

The 'four heroes' bringing out their injured mates after the Louisa Pit explosion. William Younger is at the rear (left) of the image. Younger, described as 'the last survivor' of the quartet of rescuers in his *Times* obituary, passed away in 1993 aged 83. Harry Robinson's obituary appeared in *The Times* a few years earlier, in 1987, after he died aged 70. John Hutchinson died at Stanley in 1975 aged 67.

Chapter Six

1950-1959
A Great Escape and the Last Major Disasters

The number, scale and frequency of disasters in British coal mines continued to reduce during the 1950s, as did the number of day-to-day fatalities. At the end of the decade the annual accident death toll was below 350, a great improvement of the dire situation a generation or two earlier. Apart from the 1966 Aberfan tragedy, the 1950s was the last decade in British coalmining history in which disasters of more than fifty deaths occurred.

However, in his presidential speech to the NUM's annual conference in 1953, Sir William Lawther reminded delegates, politicians and the public as a whole that 52,346 men and boys had been killed in British mines during the twentieth century, equivalent to over a thousand deaths every year.

In all fairness to 'progress', the annual fatality figures were always distorted when a major disaster occurred and this was the case in 1950 at Creswell, Derbyshire (80 deaths); and in 1951 at Easington, Durham (83 deaths), each making a significant contribution to the death total for these years (493 and 487).

There were a number of changes and introductions that would make mining a much safer place of work. From 1st January 1957 the long-awaited Mines and Quarries Act provided much tighter and new safety regulation. A new portable breathing device generally known as a 'self-rescuer' was piloted at several mines and would soon be part of every miner's kit when working underground. Safety boots and safety helmets were issued by the NCB free of charge to all miners as part of a protective clothing agreement with the NUM. The NUM also established its own National Safety Department. In 1954, in the wake of increasing mechanization, a new research and development unit was established at Bretby in Derbyshire. In the same year the NCB carried out a joint exercise with the Royal Navy at Winton Colliery in East Lothian, involving divers exploring a flooded roadway. An extremely important social and welfare innovation for miners was the establishment of the Coal Industry Welfare Organisation (CISWO) in 1951. And from 1958, the minimum age at which boys were allowed to work underground (apart from when training) was changed to sixteen years. All these developments provided the foundation for the future health and safety in the mining industry.

At the same time, however, the 1950s was also the beginning of a long period of mine closures by the NCB, the number of persons employed in the industry falling well below 700,000 by 1959. This contraction caused a great deal of unrest and uncertainty for tens of thousands of families in coalfield communities.

Once again, the bravery of individual miners and rescue teams were 'in the news' nationwide, perhaps no more so than at the extraordinary rescue of the 116 men got out of Knockshinnoch Castle Colliery in Ayrshire, following a great inrush of peat and moss, the event covered widely in the regional, national and international press and in cinemas via Pathe News. It was also 'immortalised' afterwards in the film *The Brave Don't Cry* (1952) and Arthur and Mary Selwood's *Black Avalanche* book (1960). Knockshinnoch may have been unexpected but in some respects it was a 'repeat' of the events at Donibristle (1901) and Stanrigg (1918) a generation or so earlier.

The Scottish coalfields experienced four disasters in the 1950s – more than any other region – culminating at the Auchengeich mine when forty-seven lives were lost. 'Auchengeich' was Scotland's worst pit disaster of the twentieth century, with seven more fatalities than at Redding back in 1923.

Timeline of mine disasters fatalities (5+), 1950-59

Disaster	Fatalities
7 September 1950: **Knockshinnoch**, New Cumnock, Ayrshire: (inrush)	13
26 September 1950: **Creswell,** Derbyshire: (fire)	80
29 May 1951: **Easington**, West Hartlepool, Durham: (explosion)	83
6 July 1951: **Eppleton**, Hetton-le-Hole, Durham: (explosion)	9
1 October 1951: **Weetslade**, Northumberland: (explosion)	5
4 July 1952: **Point of Ayr**, Dee Estuary: (sinking)	6
6 September 1955: **Blaenhirwaun**, Cross Hands, Carmarthen: (explosion)	6
22 November 1956: **Lewis Merthry**, Pontyprid, Glamorgan: (explosion)	9
21 February 1957: **Sutton,** Mansfield, Nottinghamshire: (explosion)	5
6 March 1957: **Chanters**, Atherton, Lancashire: (explosion)	8
26 June 1957: **Barnburgh**, Doncaster, Yorkshire: (explosion)	6
19 November 1957: **Kames,** Muirkirk, Ayrshire: (explosion)	17
14 December 1957: **Lindsay,** Cowdenbeath, Fife: (explosion)	9
22 April 1959: **Walton**, Wakefield, Yorkshire: (explosion)	6
18 September 1959: **Auchengeich**, Chryston, Lanarkshire: (fire)	47
15 October 1959: **Bickershaw**, Leigh, Lancashire: (heating)	5

Tears and elation at Knockshinnoch Castle Colliery

These days we have become more aware of the sudden appearance of 'sink holes' and flash floods in the wake of periods of continuous and torrential rain, but what happened above and below the Knockshinnoch mine at New Cumnock, in Ayrshire on a September night in 1950 was extraordinary in its scale and outcome. After many hours of heavy rain, a hollow in a farmer's field above the mine under which stood a glacial lake was penetrated by a small hole and – during an attempt to fence it off – became a great cavity through which many thousands of tons of liquid peat fell into the shallow workings below. Six miners working near the pit bottom managed to escape, eleven others were killed immediately and two lost their lives shortly afterwards, leaving 116 others trapped underground. What followed over two long days in increasingly toxic and dangerous conditions is generally regarded as the greatest and most successful rescue operation in British coalmining history.

The great (c.two-acre) crater in the field above Knockshinnoch Colliery, photographed a few days after the inrush of peat, after the engineers Wimpey had made an access route from the main road. From The Knockshinnoch Story in *Coal News* (Sept., 1950).

Knockshinnoch's modest hero

Andrew Houston, the back shift overman at Knockshinnoch Castle Colliery was a key figure in the rescue operations. It was Houston who had inspected and acted so promptly on the developing problems above and below ground, eventually finding himself trapped alongside his fellow miners. Thanks to an intact underground phone line he was able to keep in communication with his superiors and rescue people, and at the same time work tirelessly to keep the men as calm as possible. The meticulous and accurate notes that he kept during the long hours underground are also testimony to his great care and attention to every detail. His leadership was heralded in heroic terms by the press and commented on as being 'in very high order' in Sir Andrew Bryan's report of the formal investigation in to the disaster. Houston referred to his role in more modest terms, saying 'I was just doing the job I was entitled to do.'

Andrew Houston was the subject (No. 50) of the artist H.A. Freeth's much acclaimed 'pit profiles', featuring in the June 1951 edition of the NCB's *Coal News* magazine.

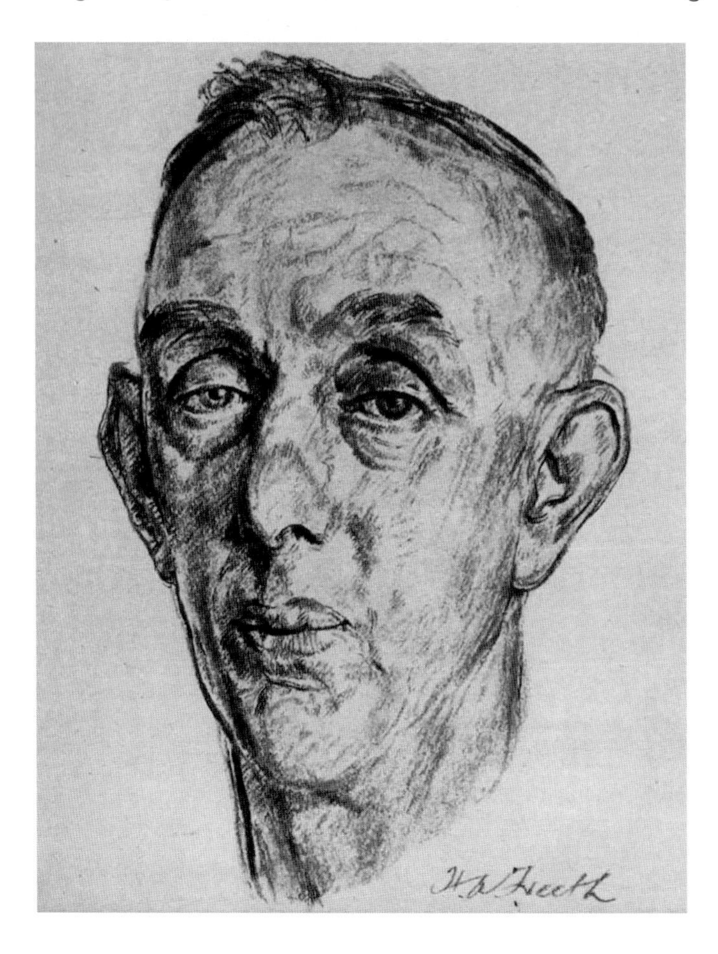

There was never any shortage of volunteers at Knockshinnoch, men in hutches (small wagons) can be seen in this photograph approaching the entrance to the old Bank drift entrance, friends and relatives in close attendance.

This rare image shows anxious relatives mingling with pit officials and rescue men at the pithead of Knockshinnoch Castle Colliery, and what appears to be an ambulance parked in the background. Note the press photographer on the right, stood next to a boy, in an elevated position, snapping images of the scene.

At first sight, David Park, who had the rather grand title of Deputy Director of Labour for NCB Scottish Division, in which Knockshinnoch was located – an administrative rather than practical job – was an unlikely volunteer to go underground via the West Mines and then communicate directly with Houston and the trapped miners. With a small rescue team, wearing Proto breathing apparatus, he managed to crawl through to the men and remained with them, explaining how important it was to 'stay put' until the gas situation had been resolved – rather than 'make a dash' for safety. But when Park discovered increasing levels of firedamp accumulating, something urgent had to be tried. And the deteriorating condition of a Bevin Boy, Gibb McAughtrie, was causing great concern. The latter was stretchered away but the route to safety was far from easy, and his escape was aided by a 'last resort' use of a 'Salvus' breathing aid. This action was what was also needed, that is to deploy borrowed Salvus apparatus for all the men; and a plan to exit in chains of three at a time 'in descending ages' and accompanied by volunteer rescue teams was executed with success – over anxious seven hours.

Park, on the right of the image shown below, is seen with his friend Andrew Houston. Both men were awarded George medals for the part they played in the rescue.

'The most daring pit rescue ever ...'

One of the trapped miners of Knockshinnoch is being supported by two rescue men a few yards after reaching the surface, a comforting cigarette in his mouth. This, another rare image, one of the more dramatic pictures taken by an unknown photographer on the day, was provided by a press agency for American newspapers. The 'strap line' was: 115 MINERS ALL SAVED: THE MOST DARING PIT RESCUE EVER.

Less than three weeks after Knockshinnoch, the eyes of the media focused on the close-knit pit community of Creswell, in Derbyshire. An underground fire broke out at about 4 am in the colliery, leaving eighty men hopelessly trapped between the ignition its aftermath and the coalface. After the deployment of rescue teams, a joint statement (from the miners, managers and inspectors) was issued stating that there was 'no possibility of any of the the men remaining in the districts affected being alive'. What a disheartening impact this must have had on the gathered crowd, the information quickly dispersed by the media. This front page detail from the *Nottingham Evening Post*, and printed on the day of the disaster, was kept by a local family for many years.

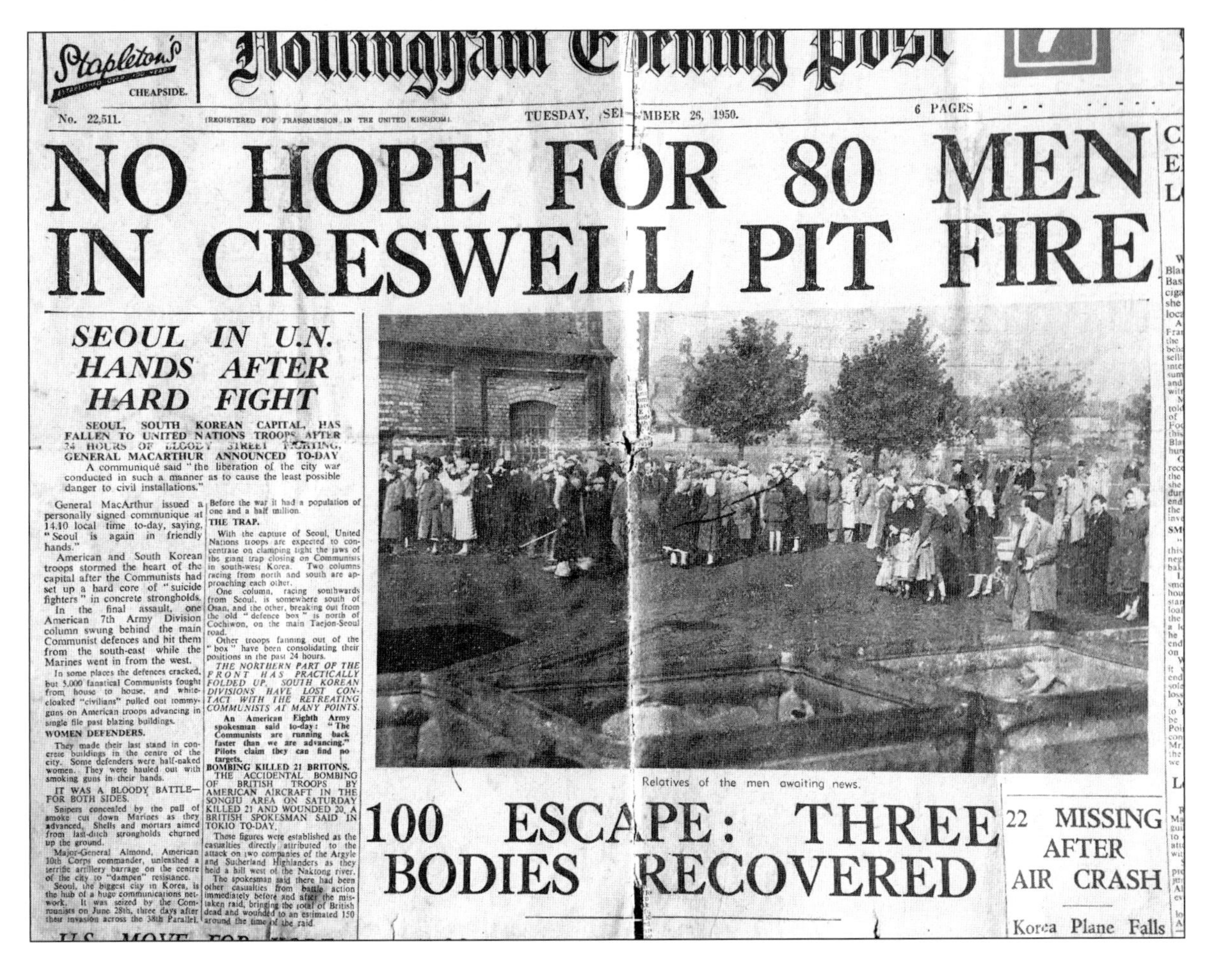

Stapleton's CHEAPSIDE.

Nottingham Evening Post

No. 22,511. (REGISTERED FOR TRANSMISSION IN THE UNITED KINGDOM.) TUESDAY, SEPTEMBER 26, 1950. 6 PAGES

NO HOPE FOR 80 MEN IN CRESWELL PIT FIRE

SEOUL IN U.N. HANDS AFTER HARD FIGHT

SEOUL, SOUTH KOREAN CAPITAL, HAS FALLEN TO UNITED NATIONS TROOPS AFTER 24 HOURS OF BLOODY STREET FIGHTING, GENERAL MACARTHUR ANNOUNCED TO-DAY

A communiqué said "the liberation of the city war conducted in such a manner as to cause the least possible danger to civil installations."

General MacArthur issued a personally signed communique at 14.10 local time to-day, saying, "Seoul is again in friendly hands."

American and South Korean troops stormed the heart of the capital after the Communists had set up a hard core of "suicide fighters" in concrete strongholds.

In the final assault, one American 7th Army Division column swung behind the main Communist defences and hit them from the south-east while the Marines went in from the west.

In some places the defences cracked, but 5,000 fanatical Communists fought from house to house, and white-cloaked "civilians" pulled out tommy-guns on American troops advancing in single file past blazing buildings.

WOMEN DEFENDERS.

They made their last stand in concrete buildings in the centre of the city. Some defenders were half-naked women. They were hauled out with smoking guns in their hands.

IT WAS A BLOODY BATTLE—FOR BOTH SIDES.

Snipers concealed by the pall of smoke cut down Marines as they advanced. Shells and mortars aimed from last-ditch strongholds churned up the ground.

Major-General Almond, American 10th Corps commander, unleashed a terrific artillery barrage on the centre of the city to "dampen" resistance.

Seoul, the biggest city in Korea, is the hub of a huge communications network. It was seized by the Communists on June 28th, three days after their invasion across the 38th Parallel. Before the war it had a population of one and a half million.

THE TRAP.

With the capture of Seoul, United Nations troops are expected to concentrate on clamping tight the jaws of the giant trap closing on Communists in south-west Korea. Two columns racing from north and south are approaching each other.

One column, racing southwards from Seoul, is somewhere south of Osan, and the other, breaking out from the old "defence box" is north of Cochiwon, on the main Taejon-Seoul road.

Other troops fanning out of the "box" have been consolidating their positions in the past 24 hours.

THE NORTHERN PART OF THE FRONT HAS PRACTICALLY FOLDED UP. SOUTH KOREAN DIVISIONS HAVE LOST CONTACT WITH THE RETREATING COMMUNISTS AT MANY POINTS.

An American Eighth Army spokesman said to-day: "The Communists are running back faster than we are advancing." Pilots claim they can find no targets.

BOMBING KILLED 21 BRITONS.

THE ACCIDENTAL BOMBING OF BRITISH TROOPS BY AMERICAN AIRCRAFT IN THE SONGJU AREA ON SATURDAY KILLED 21 AND WOUNDED 20, A BRITISH SPOKESMAN SAID IN TOKIO TO-DAY.

These figures were established as the casualties directly attributed to the attack on two companies of the Argyle and Sutherland Highlanders as they held a hill west of the Naktong river.

The spokesman said there had been other casualties from battle action immediately before and after the mistaken raid, bringing the total of British dead and wounded to an estimated 150 around the time of the raid.

Relatives of the men awaiting news.

100 ESCAPE: THREE BODIES RECOVERED

22 MISSING AFTER AIR CRASH

Korea Plane Falls

Relatives and friends listen as the latest bulletin is read out a few hours after the Creswell fire, on 26 September 1950.

This sort of scene, of families, especially women and young children waiting in the pit yard, had occurred many times in a variety of sad settings since Victorian times. Only the fashions and the locations change, this image captured by a photographer from the *Sheffield Star* who was covering the Creswell disaster, on Tuesday, 26 September 1950.

There was never a shortage of volunteers after pit disasters. Here in this image, men of all ages – and a few boys – fill sandbags after the Creswell fire, for use underground in order to help seal off the dangerous gas-infested workings. Although more than fifty bodies were recovered fairly quickly, it took until August 1951, almost a year later, for the last of the deceased miners to be recovered, the colliery having 'opened again' a few weeks earlier. The ignition was caused by the frictional heating of torn belting, according to the official inquiry; and many of the miners in the affected district would have been overcome by the noxious 'afterdamp'.

Most of the 80 miners who lost their lives in the disaster lived in the village of Creswell itself, the scene of so many funerals in the days and weeks afterwards. A commemorative window in honour of all the deceased men was placed in the parish church in 1952 and a year later an obelisk-style memorial erected and unveiled in the village cemetery. The obelisk forms the centrepiece of a discrete but specially designated area for the disaster victims and a place of quiet and respectful remembrance for their families to visit, especially on annual commemorations. The monument includes plaques inscribed with the names and ages of the miners, including several from the same families. Close by are a number of family graves relating to individual miners, the area shown in the images displayed above.

Coal News' coverage of the Easington disaster in its July 1951 edition included this front-cover tribute image showing the pit banner held high, preceded by the colliery band and followed by marching miners. Look carefully and 'a black drape of mourning' can be seen on the upper part of the banner.

Even after more than 65 years, most people with Easington associations will be aware of the disaster at the colliery that gave the pit village its name; and there may be some who can actually remember or even witnessed the terrible events of 29 May 1951, when 81 miners and two rescue workers were killed in Britain's last major mining tragedy, and the worst in Durham since the West Stanley explosion in 1909.

The blast that occurred in the 'Duckbill' area of the mine was so loud that a young pit-bottom worker, Ronnie Ritchie, said that his ears 'nearly burst with the roar', even though he was well over a mile away. Houghton-le-Spring mine rescue station was 'actioned' as were professional and volunteer teams from the neighbourhood. They rushed to the colliery and did what they could to access the trapped miners in dreadful underground conditions that included gas-filled areas and blocked roadways. Two rescuers, Henry Burdess (of Brancepeth Colliery, 43) and John Wallace (Easington, 26) collapsed and died, despite their use of breathing apparatus. But the work continued, some 295 rescue men involved in total, according to *Coal News*; and by 8 June they had made 235 explorations. It was the longest sustained operation of its kind, despite little or no hope for the 81 missing men.

MINERS TRAPPED AFTER PIT EXPLOSION

14 BODIES FOUND : OVER 60 MEN MISSING

Sixty-six men are trapped in Easington colliery, County Durham, where a violent explosion occurred early yesterday morning.

Last night the National Coal Board issued a list of 81 men dead or unaccounted for. This includes 14 bodies which were found, and one injured man who was brought to the surface but died later.

Rescue teams, working under great difficulties, were trying to reach the trapped men last night. One of the rescue workers lost his life.

Mr. E. H. D. Skinner, chairman of the Durham division of the National Coal Board, stated late last night that it would be in the nature of a miracle if any number of men were got out alive.

The King sent a message of sympathy to Mr. Skinner expressing the deepest distress of the Queen and himself on learning of the disaster.

HOPES FADING

RESCUERS DELAYED

a mobile wireless van on the surface. During the day they were reinforced, until 12 visiting teams and many volunteers from this pit were taking it in turns, trying to clear a way to the scene of the explosion. Some bodies were found at a loading point nearly half a mile ... Beyond that a heavy fall was encountered, a...

A typical headline, published the day after the disaster.

Numerous images of the Easington rescue teams appeared in national and regional newspapers. Rescue workers from the Shotton team are pictured in this example, at the surface following the disaster, a young local miner at the front carrying water bottles.

Lord (John Scott) Hyndley (1883-1963), chairman of the NCB (by the right doorway) addresses people and press at Easington in the immediate aftermath of the disaster. After giving his sympathy to relatives and praising the rescue teams, Hyndley's other comments included the saddest of news: 'Though everything has been done and is still being done, there is now no hope of any of the men being alive. This is the worst pit disaster we have had in the history of the National Coal Board.' A former Bank of England and Powell Duffryn (collieries) director, Hyndley was appointed as the first chairman of the NCB by the new Clem Attlee government in 1947. He retired from his post shortly after the Easington disaster, succeeded by Sir Hubert Houldsworth.

One of the first public memorials for the Easington disaster took the form of avenue of 83 saplings, planted ten months later, in a dell near the miners' welfare. The ceremonial covering of the roots included an imaginative pairing of 'gardeners': Easington's oldest (Bill Monk, 69) and youngest (John Liddle, 16) miners. The youngest pit lad to loose his life in the 29 May 1951 explosion was 18-year-old Matthew Williams.

The cause of the ignition of firedamp in Easington Colliery was through friction of coal-cutter picks 'on pyrites', the resultant spark-fed explosion propagated by coal dust, according to the Chief Inspector of Mines' report, published in September 1952. Only five weeks after Easington, an explosion at the nearby Eppleton Colliery, on 6 July 1951, resulted in nine deaths, the dependants 'absorbed' into the Easington relief fund. Again, it was a 'coal-dust related' explosion but on this occasion originating in the operation of an American 'Joy Loader' machine.

A Garden of Remembrance

From Easington's narrow, hillside streets, from nearby villages and from all over Durham came relatives, neighbours, and comrades of those who had lost their lives in the explosion of May, 1951.

They walked through the cemetery gates, where the Lodge banner, draped in black, was pitched, to the communal grave which is now part of a garden of remembrance for the 83 who died during the explosion and the rescue operations that followed. There, while the pit band played the solemn anthem of mining, 'Gresford', they stood with bowed heads.

Down by the shore there was the murmur of steam from the pit. In the hillside garden, with the NCB flag fluttering at half mast, there were no set speeches but only a few simple and telling words from Durham Divisional chairman E. H. D. Skinner, Durham NUM secretary Sam Watson, Emanuel Shinwell, MP., and the Rev. A. R. Beddoes, Provost of Derby, who had returned to his old parish to preside at the ceremony.

The two memorial tablets were unveiled in turn by E. H. D. Skinner and Sam Watson. Wreaths were laid by representatives of local organisations.

A Garden of Remembrance was 'opened' in a cemetery ceremony, the occasion described in some detail in the July 1954 edition of *Coal News*. As the pit band played the miners' hymn Gresford and the Easington banner dipped slightly, many heads were respectfully bowed in honour of the 83 who lost their lives, many of them interred in the adjacent communal grave. The formal unveiling of two memorial tablets and the laying of wreaths completed the solemnest of occasions.

One of the last multiple-death sinking accidents took place in north Wales at the Point of Ayr Colliery on 4 July 1952, when six men lost their lives. The colliery was undergoing redevelopment, a new shaft being created so as to enable access to deeper seams. At the time the pit was also making good use of its waste methane gas (dreaded 'firedamp'), piping it via boreholes to the colliery boilers as a 'free energy' source. Point of Ayr was so successful that it continued in production until 1996. Shaft-sinking was evident in the image to the right, just behind and to the right of the existing shaft headgears. Below is a modern photograph showing one of its winding wheels, now forming part of a memorial garden at Meliden, along the coast road to Prestatyn.

Among the mostly single-figure fatality disasters during the 1950s, was a most unusual occurrence at Sutton Colliery, near Mansfield, Nottinghamshire, in 1957. A large stone, falling from the roof of a longwall face roadhead, landed on a terminal box, the sparks setting off an explosion of firedamp. Five men were killed and twenty-five others seriously burned in the resultant fire. A memorial to the disaster victims, in the form of a carved wood sculpture, was erected outside the Brierley Forest Park's visitor centre. This image shows relatives and friends of the deceased at part of the restored memorial: (left to right) Maureen Tomlinson, Robert Reeves, Marjory Portas (a hospital nurse), Shaun Potter, Elizabeth Godber and Malcolm Godber.

Just when the 1950s were ending, on Friday 18 September 1959, tragedy struck Auchengeich colliery in Lanarkshire when 47 men died in Scotland's worst disaster for several generations. A bogie train carrying 48 miners was hauled back towards the pit bottom, from the end of its underground run, after the men frantically signalled the presence of thick smoke and dangerous fumes. Unfortunately their vehicle came to a standstill 300 yards from safety and only one man, Tom Green, managed to escape alive. The permanent rescue corps from Coatbridge fought the underground fire, backed up by voluntary brigades but all to no avail in terms of saving further life. The trapped men were immediately overcome by carbon monoxide fumes. A faulty electrically-driven booster fan proved to be the source of the fire. By 1960 the disaster fund had reached £172,000, to be accessed by the 111 dependants. A memorial to the disaster in the form of a life-size bronze 'head-bowed' miner – created by John McKenna – was unveiled by Scotland's First Minister Alex Salmond in 2009, outside the miners' welfare. Stolen shortly afterwards, the figure was replicated a year later in a respectful ceremony in the memorial gardens.

A team of determined rescue workers at Auchengeich colliery, their breathing apparatus attached to their chests.

Chapter Seven

1960-1969

South Wales, Silverwood and Scotland

The 1960s was the safest period for miners since reasonably accurate records began a century earlier. Accident fatality numbers fell from 317 at the start of the decade to 100 in 1969 (Health & Safety Executive figures), and there were only six disasters involving five or more fatalities. However, the three very serious explosions at Six Bells, Tower and Cambrian collieries in South Wales resulted in significant numbers of deaths (45, 9 and 31 respectively), telling and lasting reminders of the great historic mine disaster toll from this area, and the Aberfan tragedy, though not a mining disaster as such, cast a great shadow on the legacy of Welsh mining.

The disasters that occurred at collieries in Lancashire (Hapton Valley), Yorkshire (Silverwood) and Michael (Fife) were serious enough as to merit special inquiries or reports, and new regulations.

Although not classed as 'disasters', there were also serious multiple-fatality accidents due to explosions and gas emissions at several collieries in the early 1960s: Cardowen (1960, Lanarkshire: 4 deaths); Cortonwood (1961, Yorkshire: 4); Barony (1962, Ayr: 4); Fenton (1963, Staffs: 3) and Cefn Park (1964, S.Wales: 3).

By 1971, most of the coal produced from NCB mines (around 90%) was from mechanized faces. This introduction of heavy machinery meant that the miners, officials and safety officers had to deal with the potential of serious injury involving, for example, limbs, fingers and toes.

In part, the reduction in the number of disasters and everyday fatal accidents should also be seen in the context of a great contraction of the coal industry in the 1960s. Prime Minister Harold Macmillan's appointment of the Labour MP, Alfred Robens, shadow cabinet spokesman on industrial affairs, as chairman of the NCB in February 1961, heralded a great wave of pit closures. About 400 mines or one in every two jobs vanished in what Robens later described as his 'ten-year stint' at the Coal Board. The number of state-controlled collieries fell from 698 in 1960 to less than 300 in 1969, with an associated fall in employment, from 622,000 to 326,000. Many of the miners that remained in the industry therefore had recent experience of one or more closed pits.

As usual, it was the disasters that attracted the greatest media attention, and with television ownership becoming commonplace, visual and sound news of each tragedy reached homes over much of the country within a few hours.

Timeline of mine disaster fatalities (5+) 1960-69

28 June 1960: **Six Bells (Arrael Griffin)**, Abertillery, Mons: (explosion)	45
22 March 1962: **Hapton Valley**, Burnley, Lancashire : (explosion)	16
12 April 1962: **Tower, Hirwain**, Glamorgan : (explosion)	9
17 May 1965: **Cambrian**, Clydach, Rhondda : (explosion)	31
3 February 1966: **Silverwood**, Rotherham, South Yorks : (paddy mail)	10
[21 October 1966: **Aberfan**, Glamorgan : (tip slide)	144]
9 September 1967: **Michael**, Fife: (fire)	9

These two graphic images capture the anguish of the people from Abertillery, and the Ebbw Fach valley, especially the women who rushed to Six Bells Colliery and peered through or over the iron railings, that enclosed part of the pit yard, on Monday, 28 June 1960, 'silently waiting for news'. They were 'summoned' by 'word of mouth' rather than the sound of the explosion, despite contrary reports in the press. Mining communities, even those serving pits with excellent safety records, were highly sensitive to any information conveyed to them that indicated that something was amiss, responding immediately. At about 8pm an NCB announcement confirmed to a hushed crowd that thirty-seven bodies had been found and that there was little hope of finding the remaining eight miners alive.

Six Bells, or Arrael Griffin Colliery before nationalisation, was sunk by John Lancaster & Company in 1891. In the 1960s it had a workforce of about 1,500 and had a good safety record. The explosion occurred at about 10.45 am in the 'W' district of the mine, well over a mile from the pit bottom, forty-five of the forty-eight men working in this area losing their lives. Recalling the tragedy many years later, Jim Watkins' remarks, posted on the 'WalesOnline' site (22.9.11 & 23.2.13), included:

> 'We were told to exit the mine as quickly as possible and as we came to the top you could see the stacking of the stretchers.'

Jim was very lucky to escape, as he was dispatched to another part of the mine – and not the ill-fated 'W' or 'Old Coal Seam' area – unlike his workmate, a 19-year-old lad, who lost his life there.

Twenty-six of the miners who died were buried on the same day, a mile-long procession, some 5,000 people showed their respects alongside the widows and relatives of the deceased. The sorrowful scene was well reported visually by the *Western Mail and Echo* and by John Sullivan in his book *A Photographic History of Mining in South Wales* (2001).

Six Bells, Lancaster Pit.

Gwent's worst post-war mining disaster was commemorated in 2010 by the 'unveiling' of a 20-meter-high statue, a wonderful '50th-year' tribute to the miners who were killed in the Six Bells disaster. It was designed by Sebastian Boyesen, and described in *The Guardian* as the 'Welsh answer to Antony Gormley's Angel of the North'. The miner's body and form is made of entwined steel ribbons and overlooks the Ebbw Fach, one of the most spectacular aspects for any memorial of its kind, and forms part of the Parc Arrael Griffin's 'new landscape' and 'mining experience', combining heritage with optimism for the future. It is a wonderful composition, and a tangible point and setting where relatives and descendants of the forty-five who lost their lives can pay their respects, individual names being wrapped around the stone column that supports the statue.

Miners form a huddle below the distinctive headgear of Tower Colliery, at Hirwaun near Aberdare on 12 April 1962 but there was little that they could do to help their eight workmates who were killed outright and one man who was fatally injured. Nine other of their mates received serious injuries following the explosion in the MC3 roadway at about 10.30 that morning. A co-operation of workers took over Tower in 1994, keeping the pit going until 2008. The 1962 accident remained the worst in the colliery's long history.

Always the grimmest of jobs: rescue men stretcher a body of one of the Tower Colliery, a blanket respectfully covering the deceased miner.

These headlines were typical of those that appeared after the disaster, this example taken from *The Times*, 13 April 1962. The explosion was caused due to an ignition of gas from the short circuiting of a newly inserted cable, which had been 'bent back on itself' when connected to the a switch in the heading, weakening it's insulation, according to the mine inspector's report. Beforehand, the ventilation fan had had to be switched off in order to extend the power cable into the heading, as it was on the same power source as the rest of the machinery. New regulations concerning the powering and operation of auxiliary fans were recommended, ensuring that such accidents should never happen again.

NINE DEAD IN WELSH PIT EXPLOSION

GAS IGNITED WHILE MEN AT BREAK

From Our South Wales *Correspondent*

ABERDARE, APRIL 12

Nine men were killed and nine injured in an explosion 1,200ft. underground at Tower colliery, near Aberdare, today. Without warning, gas appears to have become ignited while some of the men were taking their midmorning break

Cambrian Colliery in Clydach Vale, near Tonnypandy in the Rhondda: the afternoon of 17 May 1965. Three valiant rescue men, their breathing apparatus strapped to their chests in the usual way and cap lamps in place, were 'snapped' by an agency press photographer. The brigade man with the blackened face, looking directly at the camera, perhaps sums up a feeling of massive disappointment equally tinged with annoyance at been photographed on an occasion when 'rescue' had become 'body recovery'; thirty-one in all from the Pentre Seam, reached via the No.1 shaft. Porth Central Mine Rescue Station had been alerted at 1.05pm, their permanent brigade led by L.C.Lewis. These courageous men were down the pit by 1.25 and at the affected district just after 2pm, having to turn back to base an hour later. After the atmosphere cleared sufficiently for a second exploration, the bodies were recovered. Among them, was the mine's young manager Ernest John Breeze (38) and the experienced undermanager of No.1 pit, Leslie James Williams (54). Most died from the carbon monoxide, the rest as a result of the 'violence' of the blast. One man, Thomas Rees (62) was described as 'seriously injured'.

A handwritten list of twenty-nine of the men who lost their lives in the Cambrian disaster, including their ages and places of residence, was carefully compiled shortly afterwards and posted for information at the colliery entrance. Added at the end were the names of the pit manager and undermanager, who were also killed.

NAME	ADDRESS	AGE
A. Colcombe.	87, Marian St Clydach. V.	44
D. Evans.	4, Bryntawel. Blnclydach	28
W.I. Thomas.	13, Francis St Clydach Vale	
L. May.	347, Brithwenydd Trealaw	33
A. Newman.	3, Bryn Terr. Blaenclydach	46
I. Jacobs.	83, Ynyscynon Rd. Trealaw	45
J. Channing.	31, Brook St. Williamstown	46
E.L. Rees.	57, Edmundstown Rd. Penrhiwfer	48
V. Nicholas.	53, Maddock St. Bl'nclydach	51
R. Daniels.	108, Park St, Clydach Vale	34
G. Thomas	31, Jones St. Bloenclydach	28
I. Morgan	Flat 2 New Century Rd. Trealaw	32
D. Price	4 Llwynypia Rd. Tonypandy	42
T. Williams	78 High St Clydach Vale	27
R.J. Roberts	25 Court St. Tonypandy	55
S. Williams	74 Ely St 〃	
K. Davies	8 Railway Terr Blaenclydach	26
E. Williams	17. Rowling St. Williamstown	51
E.W Burnett	30 Caeglass Penrhiwfer	46
T.J. Harris	4 Sunny Bank Blaenclydach	
R. Hucker	103 Park St Clydach Vale	
R Flower	83 Marian St 〃	45
D. Calvert	96 Charles St Tonypandy	40
D. Griffith	〃	43
R. Gregson	154 Dunraven St. Treherbert	21
H. Lee	70 High St. Clydach Vale	56
R. Arnold	26 Pontypridd. Rd. Porth	48
H. Pope	106 Wern St. Clydach Vale	50
G. Davies	170 Court St. Tonypandy	24
E. Breeze	[Manager]	
L. Williams	[Undermanager]	

Readers with direct experience of losing someone in a mine accident or disaster will always remember. It is perhaps not surprising that this 'memory' passes down the generations, little watered down over the years. In 2014-15 Ceri Thompson, Curator of Big Pit National Coal Museum at Blaenafon began the process of collecting together the recollections of former Cambrian workers for the bi-lingual *Glo/Coal* magazine published by the Museum of Wales. The following brief extracts and associated images relate to the disaster of 1965, shown here in due reverence and appreciation of all those who contributed to the project.

... I could only nod my head...

As I walked from the colliery in the early hours of the following morning I could not believe the events that had unfolded. If conformation was needed there was plenty provided by the way groups of people conversed at doorways at such an unusual hour, their body language indicating that the shattering news was still reverberating in their minds as it was in mine. Some of these paused as I approached as in invitation to talk but I could only nod my head as I did at the gate to my home where a group divided to allow me to enter.

Bill Richards.

I never went underground again …

I was talking about the Bingo the night before and then it happened. It was a thud rather than a bang and then the wind came down the face and knocked me on [to] the floor, hit my helmet off my head and caused some scrapes on my face. Instead of the ventilation going up the face thick brown smoke was coming down the face. … I went to shout up the face to the next stent but got no answer. The overman or the fireman must have got the information up to the surface and we were told to leave and get back to the pit bottom – it was really all we could do as the smoke was still coming down and there was no answer from the face. We went up the pit, had a shower and were sent home. I was very shook up but there wasn't any post-traumatic stress treatment offered. I was awarded £100 compensation. I never went underground again.

Myrddin Pritchard.

...a scene I will never forget...

In the face was a scene I'll never forget, there were bodies everywhere. They had died from the gas in the positions they had been working, standing up, kneeling or bending. One man still had a sledge gripped in his hands... When the stretchers arrived we placed each one on a stretcher. We then pushed and dragged each strecher back to the conveyor, covered it with brattice cloth, and went back to the face for the next one...they were placed into drams and taken to the pit bottom.

The funeral was huge; we assembled by the New Inn...and walked to Trealoaw Cemetery led by John Gregory – a miner who was also the pastor of Bush Chapel. Thousands lined the pavements; it was a tragic day for the Rhondda...Some men were so depressed that they finished, especially if they lost friends...A year after the explosion Cambrian Colliery closed.

John Benbow.

People gather by the memorial at Clydach Vale to commemorate the 50th anniversary of the Cambrian Colliery disaster in 2015. Guests of honour included several former workers, including 83-year-old John Benbow, Alwyn Davies (87) and canteen assistant Betty Thomas (87). The service of remembrance included a minute's silence at 1 pm (the same time as the explosion), the laying of wreaths, a 'roll call of those killed, a 33-bell toll; and music by the soprano Lucy Rees and the Cambrian Male Voice Choir. The explosion had occurred sixty years after a similar event at the same colliery in 1905. For the small village of Clydach it was a devastating blow, the only redeeming feature being that it occurred at 'shift-changing', otherwise very many others may have lost their lives.

A horrendous accident occurred at Silverwood Colliery near Rotherham at 7.30 am on 3 February 1966 when a a diesel locomotive pulling supply mine cars – followed another diesel 'loco paddy mail' train which had stopped at a pass bye to allow some of its passengers to disembark. The heavily-laden supply train was unable to slow down, crashing into the stationary paddy mail now carrying forty men. Nine veteran miners aged 49-59 were killed 'outright' at the scene of devastation and another man, 53-year-old Jack Nettleship, was fatally injured. Twenty-one others were injured and those relatively unscathed badly shocked. The accident occurred on the 'back shift' otherwise, as at Cambrian, many more 'regular shift workers' might have died. Here, a shaken and injured miner, is assisted to an ambulance by one of his mates.

Pit nurses had become a vital part of the medical facilities at many collieries. One of the first 'first-aiders' to go underground and treat the injured, at what must have been a terrible scene of devastation, was Silverwood's nursing sister, Diane Adsetts. Diane assisted Fred Nettleship who had had both of his legs amputated in the crash. This image shows Diane (wearing a miner's helmet) with two other nurses, Kathleen Payne (left) and Mary Parton (right). For the popular press the involvement of the women was a situation that they had to make the most of, a *Daily Mirror* reporter referring to Sister Diane as an 'Angel of Mercy'.

Sister Iris Evans (right) and two of her medical colleagues before going underground at Oakdale Colliery in the mid 1960s. Iris had trained at Tedegar General Hospital before successfully applying for a nurse's job at Pochin Colliery in 1955, prior to moving to Oakdale and eventually serving for many years as as the Senior Nursing Officer for the entire south Wales coalfield. In 1960, Iris was on duty during the Six Bells disaster.

Nine men were asphyxiated in Scotland's biggest pit, Michael Colliery, in East Wemyss, Fife, a consequence of a disastrous fire that occurred near the shaft bottom in the early morning (Sunday) of 9 September 1967. It was very fortunate that the remainder of the underground workforce, over 300 men, were successfully evacuated from the mine, including John McArthur and John McEneany, brought to the surface by rescue men after being trapped for 12 hours. Despite a long rescue operation, the situation was so bad that three of the bodies were unable to be recovered, the shaft having to be sealed and the colliery subsequently closed by the NCB. The image and headline shown here (from *The Times*, 11 September 1967) were typical of those that appeared in the regional and national newspapers afterwards.

Disaster pit is sealed off

FROM OUR SCOTTISH CORRESPONDENT

EAST WEMYSS, FIFE, SEPT. 10

Fire was still raging underground tonight in the Michael colliery here, where nine people have died after yesterday's outbreak. A constant column of smoke rises into the air.

The National Coal Board says that the fire is a big one in a seam that is exceptionally liable to spontaneous combustion, although this was not necessarily the cause of it.

Six men died yesterday. Three, who were missing, were stated this afternoon by Mr. R. W. Parker, regional chairman of the N.C.B. have had to go cautiously because of the danger of an explosion.

About 312 men were on a routine maintenance shift when the outbreak was first detected early yesterday. The cause is still unknown.

Technical examinations went on last night and today so far as conditions permitted. Mr. D. J. Ezra, deputy chairman of the N.C.B., arrived at Edinburgh airport from London and was brought here by Mr. Parker for a tour of inspection and a conference with officials of the N.C.B., the Inspectorate of Mines, and the Scottish National Union of Mineworkers.

The three men who are now haven; Henry Morrison, aged 36, of Ruskin Crescent, Buckhaven; Alexander Henderson, aged 41, of Shore Street, Leven, and Andrew Thomson, aged 55, of Shepherd Crescent, Leven.

Nearly 12 hours after the outbreak was detected, John McArthur, of Simon Crescent, Methilhill, who was 62 yesterday, and John McEneany, aged 38, of Langside Avenue, Kennoway, emerged after being trapped. The more experienced Mr. McArthur had collapsed as he was leading Mr. McEneany through the workings.

He said later: "I felt my legs go and I told him to carry on

A number of acts of bravery were recognised after the Michael Colliery disaster. The leader of the colliery's rescue team, William Shaw, got a Queen's commendation for his bravery when recovering several trapped colleagues, despite suffering face burns; and shot-firer David Hunter, almost totally exhausted from rescue efforts, was awarded the George Medal for carrying one of his mates to safety. But the most poignant of the awards was the Edward Medal given to a deputy, Andrew Taylor, who refused to turn away from the black, choking smoke in order to find his missing men. He was never seen again.

Among the safety matters that were highlighted by the official inquiry was a new requirement for 'self-rescuers' (portable respiratory equipment) to be issued to all miners at work underground. The person largely credited for initiating this was the Scottish NUM leader, Michael McGahey (1925-1999), who was also successful in campaigning for the installation of emergency telephones at key underground locations. McGahey, later to become Vice-President of the NUM and a prominent figure in the 1984-85 strike, is shown here, along with a diagram of the self-rescuer that became 'standard issue'; and had to be carried by all miners working underground from 1973.

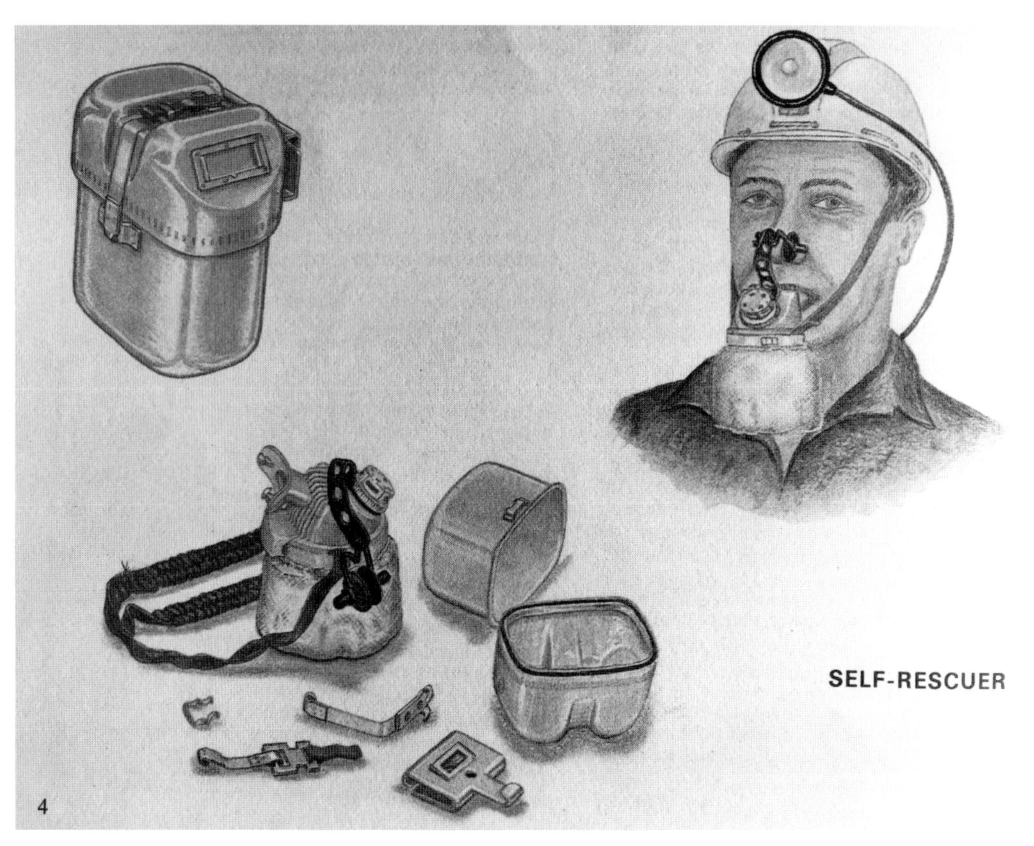

Chapter Eight

1970-1979 Britain's Last Pit Disasters: Remembering Lofthouse and Safety in Mines

In 2011 four miners lost their lives in Gleison Colliery, a small drift mine in the Swansea Valley, a stark reminder of the price of coal in the modern era. Earlier, in 1993, three men were killed following a roof collapse at Bilsthorpe in Nottinghamshire.

But historians will always refer to the 1970s as the last of the 'mine disaster decades' in British coalmining history. It was during this period that 58 men were killed in seven multiple-fatality accidents each involving five or more fatalities. This figure was almost half of the comparable total for the previous decade and there was also a significant reduction in the annual number of fatalities in British coal mines, from 91 in 1970 to 46 in 1979.

At the same time, the contraction of the industry continued apace, 'manpower' falling by 61,000 (to 243,000), a trend accelerating so fast that there were only 219 collieries in 1979-80 and 191,000 mine workers employed in 1983.

The most serious disaster of the 1970s occurred in Derbyshire at Markham Colliery. An out of control cage plummeted to the bottom of the Shonkey shaft, causing the deaths of eighteen miners. Seven men died in yet another man-riding accident in Yorkshire, this time at Bentley Colliery, near Doncaster. The same number were killed at Lofthouse Colliery, in west Yorkshire, after a inrush of water so sudden, violent and massive that it was as though an underground tsunami had struck. In Scotland, five men died due to a fall of roof at Seafield in Fife, but it was the 'most familiar of all': fires, explosions and associated gases that accounted for the other disasters, the last at Golborne in Lancashire taking ten lives.

The National Coal Board's Public Relations department continued to promote mining as a 'safety-conscious industry' and indeed a wide variety of initiatives permeated the coalfields throughout the seventies. Scientific and technical innovation was such that canaries were 'on their last legs' but the little birds would never be forgotten.

The closure of Kellingley Colliery in 2015 marked the end of deep mining in Britain, and of course the end of fatalities; the post-1984-85 miners' strike decimation of the industry under the watch of successive governments was now complete.

Timeline of mine disaster fatalities (5+), 1970-79

6 April 1971: **Cynheidre-Pentremaur**, Llanelli, Carmarthenshire : (gas)	6
21 March 1973: **Lofthouse**, Wakefield, Yorkshire: (inrush)	7
10 May 1973: **Seafield**, Fife : (roof fall)	5
30 July 1973: **Markham**, Chesterfield, Derbyshire : (winding)	18
12 June 1973: **Houghton Main**, Barnsley, Yorks: (explosion)	5
21 November 1978: **Bentley**, Doncaster, Yorks (man-riding)	7
18 March 1979: **Golborne**, Lancashire : (explosion)	10

The first disaster of the 1970s occurred in south Wales, when an outburst of methane, in combination with fine coal dust, resulted in death by asphyxia six Cynheidre miners on 6 April. At least 25 other miners were badly affected by the incident. A few years later, Michael Williams survived a terrible ordeal at this colliery, trapped underground for 23 hours, after an inrush of water had killed his workmate, Frank Evans. Williams was dubbed a 'miracle man' in the July 1973 issue of the NUM's newspaper.

Seven men died in Lofthouse Colliery near Wakefield on 21 March 1973, when a great inrush of water, from unknown workings of an old pit, burst through the Flockton Thin seam into the South 9B face and flooded roadways. Old shafts became visible on the surface of the local landscape, the inquiry confirming that the inrush had come from 'uncharted' workings from the Bye Pit and the Engine Pits of the long-abandoned Low Laithes Colliery. Despite massive and valiant round-the-clock rescue attempts the body of one man, Charles Cotton, was to be recovered after several days. The tragedy attracted widespread media attention, journalists and camera crews rushing to the pithead, seeking 'copy' and images for their editors. This image, sent to New York for news coverage in the USA, shows a large group of helmeted miners at the colliery waiting for news of their colleagues, cars parked at the base of the buildings, some of the vehicles located by a safety notice that read: DANGER, BEWARE OF MOVING WAGONS.

One of many poignant pit-top images, relating to the search and rescue operations, shows a small group of miners walking away from the shaft, several still wearing breathing apparatus. The man second right, with a 'blackened' face, looking at the photographer is Tony Banks who had been working as an overman on the night of the disaster. Tony completed his official 'life in mining' in the Selby coalfield after working in mining from the age of fifteen. But that was not the end of a long and productive link with Lofthouse, an association that has continued to the present day. With the help of small number of colleagues, Tony has been a key figure in the community for the commemoration of the disaster, including the installation of monuments and anniversary events. The Lofthouse Story has also been passed on to present and future generations via his many talks and presentations.

The search operations at Lofthouse included the use of 'mines rescue frogmen' from Hednesford in Staffordshire, miner-divers specially trained for accessing flooded pits. Trials and dives proved to be extremely difficult as well as hazardous because the water was so fouled with dirt and debris; and visibility was down to zero in places, black on black. One consequence of Lofthouse was the introduction of new regulation enabling the wider training of rescue personnel in diving skills, needed in the aftermath of inrushes in mines. Another was a national appeal for old mining plans and geological/mining engineering notebooks, in an effort to eradicate further tragedies.

This image shows several of the Hednesford team wearing wetsuits and breathing apparatus.

The images shown here are part of a rare series showing the devastation that eventually became visible following the 1973 Lofthouse inrush, a scene that will be familiar for miners in other pits that may have had experience of the sudden flooding of workings and roadways. The miner in the lower photograph is a Lofthouse surveyor, Peter Wood.

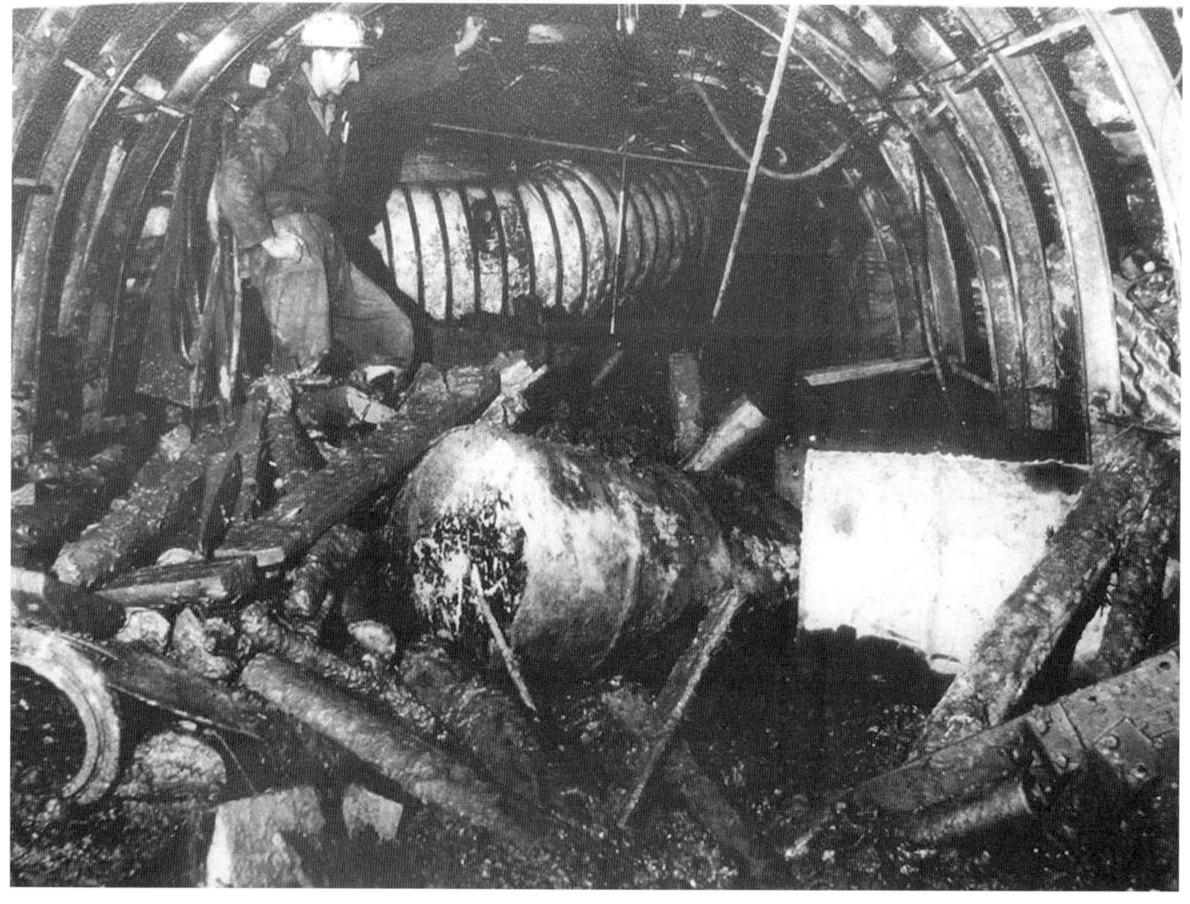

Tony Banks, one of the last survivors of the miners working at Lofthouse on that fateful shift, 21 March 1973, is shown here at the first major memorial to the disaster victims. The base of the granite obelisk is inscribed with the names and ages of each person who died, along with a commemorative dedication. Set within a memorial garden off Batley Road, Outwood, the site continues to be used for anniversary services, and a place where families, friends and anyone interested in mining heritage are able to visit and show their respects.

The smaller image shows the 'unveiling ceremony' on a rainy Sunday, 24 November 1974.

One of the most remarkable and imaginative ways in which an abandoned pit site and its environment can be transformed, commemorated and used as a recreational, educational and place of natural/wildlife importance, can now be seen at the Lofthouse Colliery Nature Park, managed by Wakefield Council. A trail has been created via the Council and hard work of local volunteers, including members of the Outwood Community Video and the Lofthouse Colliery Action Group. Also through their lottery funding initiatives, visitors can follow a dedicated heritage trail or simply walk through a pleasant landscape. It is also possible via the interpretation boards or online to download a free app and listen to the stories of former mineworkers. This image shows a small group of former miners by a relatively new (2013) park installation, an obelisk in memory of all Lofthouse workers including those who fought in two world wars. In the form of a reverse mine shaft, it stands alongside a large 5-ton 'mine car' of a similar kind to those used at Lofthouse Colliery after nationalisation. It was obtained from UK Coal's Kellingley Colliery. Left to right, the ex-miners are: Archie Paton, Tony Banks, Steven Wyatt, Eddie Downes and Stuart Heptinstall.

Lofthouse veteran Tony Banks at the site of the A shaft, which, along with B shaft, forms a part of the Lofthouse Colliery Nature Park Heritage Trail. Used for coal winding and underground ventilation, the shaft was sunk over a 3-year period, reaching the Silkstone Seam in November 1876. Brick-lined, it measured 5.6 meters across (18 feet) and reached a depth of 321m (351 yards). Lofthouse Colliery was closed by the NCB in 1981, eight years after the 'inrush disaster'.

It continues to be important for future generations that memories of miners and their families are recorded and kept in suitable and accessible museums and archives. Inevitably this will include recollections concerning accidents and disasters, occasions that, because of their very emotive nature, remain so vivid. Tony Banks, acting as an overman, was very much involved in post-disaster activities at Lofthouse, above and below ground. The following very brief extracts are based on a recording made in June 2016, over 43 years later:

> 'It was just a normal night … as we got out of the paddy the men went left to South 9B. Me and my men went down to the C4s … and the last words spoken by those lads were 'Don't you be late in the morning Banky'. I said, "Don't worry about us, just make sure you're there!" The next morning [when they weren't there] it hits you very hard..it sticks in your mind ... forever.
>
> At twenty past two – I'll remember it as long as I live – there was a sudden surge of wind – whoosh – and it knocked us over, the air had turned ...something was seriously wrong...the air started blowing again [normally] and we got cutting again and about twenty past four in the morning the labour overman told me to go to the Main Gate as there had been an inrush of water, with fourteen men unaccounted for. I had to get my men out of the pit.
>
> The first night I was back I was told to meet the mines inspector ... he was smaller than me, which takes some believing! And as we were walking [underground] I could hear him blowing bubbles and he says to me, 'Deputy, I want you to inspect for gas'. Well, my lamp was full of water, I had it round my neck and the water level was neck height! He also said why aren't you wearing wellingtons? I said to him, "Don't you remember when you was a boy paddling in the beck and getting your wellies full of water and not able to run properly?" He said, "Point taken". Wearing boots, I could walk but would still come out of the pit with my legs cut to ribbons.
>
> We had a big meeting in Outwood Empire and Sid Haigh, who had lost his son stood up and said he did not want more men to risk their lives any further … everyone who came out of that meeting felt as if a bomb had dropped … we were gutted … and the union man Jack Bennett told us later that we would be very disappointed if he had to walk through the village after more men had been lost … but Lofthouse men refused to seal the workings ... contractors had to be employed.
>
> When we got working again it was very subdued...everyone was on edge ...'

Scotland's improving day-to-day safety record received a severe jolt in 1973 when in it's largest colliery, Seafield, props and supports collapsed, killing five men. Official reports apart, some of the circumstances and background are well told by one of its former miners, Ian Terris, in his book *Twenty Years Down the Mines* (2001).

In England, despite numerous built-in safeguards, eighteen mineworkers lost their lives in a freak overwind at Markham Colliery, near Chesterfield, the extraordinary image shown below shows the tangled rope and damaged cage that careered 440 yards to the pit bottom. The two-decked 'lift' contained 29 men, all eleven of the survivors receiving serious injuries and another man was badly injured in the rescue operation. The failed braking system resulted in the cage smashing into the roof of the engine house and also damaging an adjacent workshop prior to its final and horrific plunge. The shocked winding engine man Dick Kennan did what he could in the circumstances and narrowly escaped death and injury himself under a shower of falling masonry. The damaged cage with its tangled ropes can be seen in this image.

Derbyshire miners carry one of their deceased colleagues away from the affected shaft at Markham Colliery in 1973, a scene that took place on so many other occasions throughout much of the twentieth century.

The 1970s was a period when the NCB continued its campaign to improve health and safety in mines, adopting a variety of schemes. These included 'safety drives', with associated posters displayed at pitheads, this example believed to be at Whitwell in Derbyshire, only a few months after the Markham tragedy. NCB photographers were dispatched to pits to capture images that would appear in *Coal News* or indeed in any publication happy to include them.

Undoubtedly the most bizarre of all the NCB's Public Relations safety initiatives was the commissioning in 1976 of 'sing-a-long' Max Bygraves (with the Grimethorpe Colliery Band) to perform on a single record *Do It The Safety Way*. The words were composed by Bickershaw Colliery's administrative officer Jack Birchall, who had won the right of publication in a competition run by *Coal News*. The concept was, apparently, adopted by the NCB's chief safety engineer John Collinson. Said to be 'an everyday musical message for mining folk', and having 'hit parade appeal' it never got any near to making the Top Ten!

An explosion at Houghton Main Colliery, near Barnsley, in the Meltonfield workings, killed five men on Thursday 12 June 1975. The blast occurred at about 6.50pm on one of the warmest days of the year. Tony Benn, the new Secretary of State for Energy, visited the scene the day after and in his comments to the media reminded everyone of the high price paid for the coal that the country needed. Arthur Scargill, the Yorkshire NUM president, as at Lofthouse, was an early underground explorer at the colliery, along with the union and several MPs he played a prominent part in campaigning for an official inquiry. Another early visitor was the chairman of the Coal Board, Sir Derek Ezra. The Houghton disaster was featured on the front page of *The Miner*, the NUM's official media 'voice'.

Miner

VOICE OF THE NATIONAL UNION OF MINEWORKERS

JUNE/JULY 1975

Explosion kills five men

THE YORKSHIRE Area of the NUM have called for a public inquiry into the explosion at Houghton Main Colliery, near Barnsley, which killed five men on Thursday, 12 June. Tony Benn, the new Secretary of State for Energy, who visited the scene of the disaster on Friday, has promised a statement in the House of Commons. He commented that the accident might remind people of the high price of life still to be paid for the coal Britain needed.

Minister Tony Benn and Yorkshire President Arthur Scargill at Houghton Main.

Bill Simpson, chairman of the Health and Safety Commission set up by the Government last October, stated that investigation would start as soon as the air in the Newhill seam—where the explosion occurred—was suitable.

A dozen men were working in the seam at the time of the explosion, preparing it for its first production which was due to start on Monday, 16 June.

The five killed were Richard Bannister, 30, a development worker; Irvin Larkin, 55, a colliery deputy; Arnold Williamson, 59, colliery deputy; Raymond Copperwheat, 42, electrician; Leonard Baker, 53, electrician. Six other men were injured.

Grade A Plus talks to continue

NUM National Officials, President Joe Gormley and Secretary Lawrence Daly, were having informal talks with the National Coal Board to continue discussion on the implementation of a Grade A Plus rate. The June meeting of the NEC heard that the Joint Working Party had had seven meetings and had visited a number of pits where installations were examined. One change in the NUM's approach was that the Grade A Plus discussions should include all solid drivages. The criteria for deciding which development headings should qualify was also under dispute, the Coal Board wanting to include a qualifying finished height of 12 feet.

Working Party on Winding

In parliament, among the MPs who spoke about the disaster were Dennis Skinner and Albert Booth, each paying tribute to the rescue teams and demanding detailed and co-operative investigations of all parties, the mines inspectorate, the NCB and the NUM. Eighty-one persons gave evidence in the 9-day public inquiry held in Barnsley Town Hall. The explosion 'resulted from the ignition of an accumulation of firedamp in B05's return development heading which had been unventilated for a period of nine days...' was the main conclusion, the ignition coming from frictional sparking of an auxiliary fan.

Grim-faced miners come to the surface at Houghton Main after the explosion in June 1975.

Twelve years after the Silverwood man-riding accident, at 4.45 am on 21 November 1978, a diesel-hauled underground train, in which 65 men were returning to the shaft bottom, ran out of control down a one-in-sixteen incline at Bentley Colliery near Doncaster. Unable to cope with a curve at the foot of the incline, the train derailed and crashed into a steel arched roadway support. Seven men lost their lives and three others were seriously injured. The Health and Safety Executive found that the driver and conductor of the vehicle had 'inadequate training' and 'there was widespread failure to comply with the mine's transport rules'. According to the Mines and Quarries Inspectorate 'no one...whether official or workman, should feel satisfied with his conduct'. Powerful diesel 'locos', such as the example illustrated here, had 'failsafe' devices incorporated in their design but the Bentley accident showed that tragedies could still occur. Little more than a year later, two men were killed in a 'runaway' man-riding accident at Kinsley Drift, a new pit, also in Yorkshire, when the safety breaking system failed.

Lancashire's and Britain's last coalmining disaster occurred at Golborne Colliery, near Wigan, on 18 March 1979. Three men were killed outright from the blast of a huge explosion and the burns and associated injuries that affected eight others were so bad that all but one, apprentice electrician Brian Rawsthorne, died in hospital later. Among the miners who helped to stretcher their colleague out of the pit was Frank Gormley, son of the NUM's president, Joe Gormley. Brian Rawsthorne read a tribute at the 35th anniversary service for the ten victims in St Thomas' Church in 2014, following a very well attended procession through Golborne. An audio clip concerning the 'disaster memories' of one of the Golborne miners, Colin Holland, can be accessed online via http://lossofface.co.uk/ golborne.htlm. Former miners Alan Mitchell, Brian Eden and Alan Parr are seen here by the side of the memorial to their Golborne colleagues. BBC Golborne (Manchester: History) archived feature: 'The death of mining in Wigan' (13.11.2014)

During the 1970s (and earlier as per this 1960s example) miners used methanometers, small, compact scientific devices when testing for gas. In this illustration the methanometer is being used in combination with a probe to take air samples near the roof of a mine. A range of methanometers and firedamp detectors/alarms were available in the 1970s, featured in various editions of the NCB booklet, *Mine Gases*.

A feathered friend: in 1981 David Kirk (pictured below) had responsibility for 22 canaries as part of his job as a rescue man at the Mansfield (Nottinghamshire) station. 'Electric sniffers' (methanometers and detectors) had just about taken over from 'bird detectors' but canaries, always trusted and held in great affection by miners, continued to be housed at many collieries until phased out by British Coal in the early 1990s. From 1954 two birds had to be kept at mines employing more than a hundred men underground as part of the fire and rescue regulations of the Mines and Quarries Act. Haldane resuscitators, with their miniature oxygen bottles, used to revive gas-affected birds, can be seen on display at mining museums. The National Mining Museum for England still has an aviary of canaries as part of its exhibits.

This limited edition plate, produced by E.J. And J.A. Downes in 1995, commemorates the Mines Rescue Service (1902-1994) and at its centre feature two rescue men wearing old and modern breathing apparatus. Just below is an illustration showing a canary resuscitation cage. The inner rim contains the names of fourteen significant twentieth-century pit disasters involving mines rescue teams, from Maypole (1908) to Bilsthorpe (1993). Printed on the outer edge are the names of 53 rescue stations that existed at various times, starting with the first, the Tankersley station, near Barnsley and and ending with the first central station, at Howe Bridge (Lancashire).

Miners' banners often include references to safety and mines rescue. But this example is dedicated entirely to the NUM Yorkshire Area's Mines Rescue Branch. This image was taken in 2006 when it was on display in the Miners' Hall, NUM headquarters, Barnsley. An oxygen container, self-rescuer, flame lamp and canary are shown at the corners of the banner, which features a rescue man wearing breathing apparatus at the centre.

Endpiece

'It's a pitiable reflection on us all that most of the improvements in safety laws over the last century have been fathered by disaster.'

Alwyn Machin, President NUM Yorkshire Area
(Final submission to the Walton Colliery disaster inquiry, 1959)

* * *

Dedication

For Rhys Elliott Jenkins

Sources and Picture Credits

Source material for anyone wanting to research 20th-century mine disasters is huge, including audio and film recordings. Of the very many internet sites, the most useful are: www.dmm.or.uk ('Durham Mining Museum': especially for northern England); www.welshcoalmines.co (for Welsh disasters); www.scottishmining.co.uk (Scottish disasters) and www.healeyhero.co.uk (mine rescue and disasters) and 'Heroes of Mine' (mine rescue) (https://sites.google.com/site/minerescuehistory/home): Philip Clifford.

Most of the illustrations and much of the background information used for this book has come from my personal archive and collection, alongside items obtained from those individuals and organisations as credited below.

Aberdeen Journal: 87; Maureen Anderson: 105,129; BBC: 168; Tony Banks Collection: 154,155,156; Barnsley Chronicle: 85,166; The Chad: 131; Pam Clarke/West Houghton Local History Group: 40; Coal News/NCMME: 113,116,124,126,127,128,129; Colliery Guardian (National Coal Mining Museum for England [NCMME]): 15, 25, 26, 28,51,110; Dundee Courier: 104; Dundee Evening Telegraph: 86; Dunfermline Press: 88; Falkirk Herald: 58; Freeth family archive: 103,114; Gloucester Echo: 104; Les Johnson: 2; Johnson Press: 95,105,106,107; Ray Johnson MBE/Staffordshire Film Archive: 100-01; Kirkintolloch Herald: 132; Leigh Journal: 102; Old Barnsley: 13; Edgar Orgill: 66; Newcastle Chronicle & Journal (dave Morton): 52,53,74; Nottingham Evening Post: 119,120; NUM:152,156,165; Public domain: 48,54,58,61,62,137,167; Scothill/GNU Free Doc: 112; Sheffield Independent: 68; Sheffield Newspapers: 121,122,146,147,162; Staffordshire Sentinel: 47; Stewart Williams Publishing: 21; Sunderland Echo: 104; Ceri Thompson/Glo/Museum of Wales: 7,79,135,141,142,143,144,145,148; Times Newspapers: 64,70,95,97,104,125; Tyrelian: 137; Western Daily Express: 95; Western Mail & Echo: 136; Whitehaven News: 108; Wigan Today: 73.

Former Yorkshire miners Archie Paton (Newmarket Colliery) and Steve Wyatt (Dodworth Colliery), both keen to keep mining heritage alive, at the new Miners' Memorial Garden, at the National Coal Mining Museum for England. For a small sum (currently £40) individuals and families can have the name of a loved one (or a mining event) inscribed on a specially-crafted glass cheque, and then placed on the memorial. Please see ww.ncm.org.uk/memorial for more information. Sadly, Archie passed away a few weeks after this photograph was taken, so the final chapter of this book is dedicated to his memory.